Charlie Tillman

Glowing songs

Charlie Tillman

Glowing songs

ISBN/EAN: 9783337266462

Printed in Europe, USA, Canada, Australia, Japan

Cover: Foto ©Thomas Meinert / pixelio.de

More available books at **www.hansebooks.com**

HOLY BIBLE

GLOWING SONGS

By

Charlie D. Tillman

Editor of THE REVIVAL SONG BOOK,

which has reached a sale of over One Hundred Thousand ⊚ ⊚ ⊙ .

✳ ✳

...PREFACE...

"GLOWING SONGS" will speak for itself
Your examination of it will be far more
satisfactory than anything I might say in its
behalf. Try it, and if it is not what you
want there are plenty others on the market.
I assure you I have done MY BEST to make
a book that will meet the present demands,
and hope it will.

Yours,

CHARLIE D. TILLMAN.

GLOWING SONGS.

"OLD TIME POWER."

C. D. T.   CHARLIE D. TILLMAN.

1. { They were gathered in an upper chamber, They were all with one ac-cord; }
   { When the Ho - ly Ghost descended, Which was promised by our Lord. }

2. { This   power from heaven de-scend-ed,   As the sound of rushing wind; }
   { Tongues of fire rested there up-on them, Je-sus prom-ised He would send. }

3. { Our fathers had this "old time" power, And we all may have it too; }
   { This He   promised to the faith-ful, What He's promised He will do. }

Chorus.

O, Lord; send the power just now,   O, Lord; send the power just now,

O, Lord; send the power just now And bap-tize   ev - 'ry   one.

LOVE FOUND ME.

H. L. GILMOUR.   Arr. by H. L. G.

1. When out in sin and darkness lost, Love found me, My fainting soul was
2. The Spir-it roused me from my sleep, Love found me, Conviction seized me
3. I'll praise Him while He gives me breath, Love found me, For sav-ing from an
4. And when I reach the gold paved street, Love found me, I'll sit a-dor-ing

tempest tossed, Love found me, I heard the Saviour's words so blest, Love found me.
strong and deep, Love found me, Al-tho' I long withstood His grace, Love found me,
endless death, Love found me, Christ is my ad-vo-cate above, Love found me,
at His feet, Love found me, And sing hosannas round the throne, Love found me,

Chorus.

Come, wea-ry, heav-y lad-en, rest, Love found me. Oh, 'twas love, love,
He wooed me to His kind embrace, Love found me.
I'm yoked to Him in perfect love, Love found me.
Where I shall know as I am known, Love found me. Oh, 'twas love, 'twas wondrous love

Love that moved the might-y God, Love, love, 'twas love found me.

EVER BE FAITHFUL.

No. 3.

E. A. H.

Rev. E. A. HOFFMAN.

1. Ev - er to Je-sus be faith-ful and true, He has been ten- der and
2. Hon- or the Master by do- ing His will, Love Him, and all His com-
3. Cling un- to Je-sus, thy Strength and thy Might, Cling in the darkness, and

faith- ful to you; Fol- low Him dai - ly what - ev - er be - tide,
mandments ful - fill; And as you jour- ney life's pil- grim- age through,
cling in the light, Hon - or His name in what - ev - er you do,

Chorus.

Fol - low your Lead - er and Guide. ⎫ Ev - - - er be
Ev - er be faith - ful and true. ⎬ Ev - er be faith - ful and
Ev - er be faith - ful and true. ⎭

faith - - ful, Ev - - - er be faith - - ful,
ev - er be true, Ev - er be faith- ful and ev - er be true,

Ev - - er be faith - - ful, Ev - - er be true.
He has been tender and faithful to you, Ev-er be faithful and true.

THE JUDGMENT.

War Cry.

CHARLIE D. TILLMAN

1. I dreamed that the great Judg-ment Morn - ing Had
2. The rich man was there, but his mon - ey Had
3. The wid - ow was there and the or - phans, God
4. The mor - al man came to the judg - ment, But his

dawned, and the trum - pet had blown; I dreamed that the
melt - ed and van - ished a - way; A pau - per he
heard and re - mem-bered their cries; No sor - row in
self - righteous rags would not do; The men who had

na-tions had gath - ered To judg-ment be- fore the white throne.
stood in the judg-ment, His debts were too heav - y to pay.
heav - en for - ev - er, God wiped all the tears from their eyes.
cru - ci - fied Je - sus, Had passed off as mor - al men too.

THE JUDGMENT. Concluded.

From the throne came a bright shin - ing an - gel And
The great man was there, but his great - ness When
The gam - bler was there and the drunk - ard, And the
The souls that had put off sal - va - tion—"Not to

D.S.—And oh, what a weep - ing and wail - ing When the

stood on the land and the sea, And swear with his
death came was left far be - hind, The an - gel that
man who had sold them the drink, With the peo - ple who
night; I'll get saved by - and - bye: No time now to

lost ones were told of their fate; They cried for the

hand raised to heav - en, That time was no long - er to be.
o-pened the rec - ords, Not a trace of his great-ness could find.
gave him the li-cense—To - geth - er in hell they did sink.
think of re - lig - ion!" At last they had found time to die.

rocks and the mount-ains, They prayed, but their pray'rs were too late.

HE WAITS FOR THEE.

Mrs. A. L. DAVISON.   J. H. FILLMORE.

1. Up-on the great high-ways thou stand-est wea - - ry,
2. The hopes of earth-life oft - en fade and fail   thee,

wea-ry, standest wea- ry,
fail thee, fade and fail thee,

Thou cri-est ev - er- more "A - lone and drear - - y,"
Thou hast no ref - uge when thy foes as - sail   thee

drear-y, lone and dreary,
- sail thee foes as-sail thee,

And wilt not un - der-stand that there so near   thee,
And when the night shall come, oh, who will guide   thee,

near thee, there so near thee,
guide thee, who will guide thee,

Thy Sav-iour waits to love, and bless, and cheer   thee.
If thou dost still re - fuse thy Friend be - side   thee.

cheer thee, bless and cheer thee.
- side thee, Friend beside thee.

HE WAITS FOR THEE.—Concluded.

* He stands so near, and yet thy blind-ed vis-ion Is
In Him is strength, in Him di-vine com-pas-sion, He

turned a-way from hope and light e-lys-ian, Thou
chang-es not, though things of earth-ly fash-ion Grow

wilt not see that 'tis for thee He car-eth, For
old and die, ah! turn thee, heart so wea-ry, And

thee, for thee the heav-y cross He bear - - - eth.
thou shalt nev-er more be lone and drear - - - y.

the heav-y cross He bear-eth.
and drear-y, lone and drear-y.

* May be repeated to the end for chorus.

No. 6.   I STOOD OUTSIDE THE GATE.

Arr. CHARLIE D. TILLMAN.

DUET.   Ten. and Sop.

1. I stood out-side the gate, A poor way-far-ing child, With-
2. Oh, "Mer-cy!" loud I cried, "Now give me rest from sin!" "I
3. In mer-cy's guise I knew The Sav-iour long a-bused, Who

in my heart there beat A tem-pest loud and wild; A fear op-
will," a voice re-plied; And mer-cy let me in, She bound my
of-ten sought my heart; And wept when I re-fused; Oh, what a

pressed my soul, That I might be too late, And oh, I troub-led sore,
bleeding wounds, And soothed my heart oppressed, She washed away my guilt,
blest re-turn For all my years of sin! I stood outside the gate

Chorus.

And pray'd without the gate.   )
And gave me peace and rest.   } Je-sus is call-ing, is call-ing, is
And Je-sus let me in.   )

call-ing, Je-sus is call-ing; Open wide your heart and let Him in.

No. 7. SCATTER SUNSHINE.

LANTA WILSON SMITH.

E. O. EXCELL.

1. In a world where sor- row Ev - er will be known, Where are found the
2. Slight-est ac-tions oft - en Meet the sor - est needs, For the world wants
3. When the days are gloomy, Sing some hap-py song, Meet the world's re -

need - y, And the sad and lone; How much joy and com - fort
dai - ly, Lit - tle kind - ly deeds; Oh, what care and sor - row,
pin - ing, With a cour-age strong; Go with faith un-daunt - ed,

You can all be- stow, If you scatter sunshine Ev'ry where you go.
You may help re- move, With your songs and courage, Sympathy and love.
Thro' the ills of life, Scat- ter smiles and sunshine, O'er its toil and strife.

Chorus.

Scat - ter sunshine all a- long your way, Cheer and bless and
Scatter the smiles and over the way,

1 bright-en Ev -'ry pass - ing day, **2** Ev -'ry pass- ing day.

No. 8.   Steer Straight to the Light-House.

T. W. D.   T. W. DENNINGTON.

1. Say where are you go - ing, my broth - er? Up - on the broad
2. Be sure that the Sav - iour is with thee Where-ev - er thy
3. Look not on the lamps that burn dim - ly ; But look to the

o - cean of   time,   Are you bound for the land of   the bless-ed,
life boat may   go,   Should you take your life journey with - out Him,
light of God's   love;   Look   not   on the wrecks by the sea-shore,

Chorus.

A home in fair Canaan's bright clime.)
You'll sink 'neath the bil-lows of   woe. } Steer straight to the lighthouse, my
But look to the lighthouse a - bove.)

broth-er, There's dan-ger up - on the dark wave,   Ask Je - sus to

keep and to guide you. He's a - ble and will-ing to   save.

No. 9. **WHOSOEVER CALLETH.**

H. H. S.

HAMP. H. SEWELL.

1. Who-so-ev-er call-eth on the Lord Hath a promise thro' His name,
2. Who-so-ev-er call-eth on the Lord By your faith ye shall re-ceive,
3. Sin-ner, hear His message 'tis for thee, Hear Him pleading for thy soul;

And e-ter-nal life shall thus be giv'n, Let us now His praise proclaim.
In His name all those who will may come, Sin-ner why not now be-lieve.
Thro' His mer-cy He did'st thou redeem, Come and let it make thee whole.

Refrain.

Who-so-ev-er call-eth, who-so-ev-er call-eth, Who-so-ev-er

call-eth on His name shall be saved, Whosoev-er call-eth, Whoso-ev-er

call-eth, Who-so-ev-er call-eth on His name shall be saved.

ONLY A DRUNKARD.

To Miss Clara Parrish, National Organizer of the Y. W. C. T. U.

A. O. B.　　　　　　　　　　　　　　　　　　　　A. Oscar Browne.

1. It was on-ly a drunkard that fell on the snow, But
2. Ah! then pick him up ten-der-ly, leave him not there, For
3. For he has a heart and a-round it may twine The
4. For her cry to her God for the child that he gave Is

he's . . . somebody's dar-ling I'd have you to know; Ah,
the heart-less to laugh at the sin-ful to jeer; Take
love . . . of a moth-er as ten-der as thine, She
"spare . . him oh, spare from a poor drunkard's grave," The

* rit.*

leave him not there To suf-fer and die, Look on the poor fel-low and
him to his mother, She'll bless you I know, Tho' 'twas on-ly a drunkard that
clings to her darling 'Tho' he causeth her grief, And tears for her child seem her
grief of such mothers God on-ly can know, He pit-ies these drunkards that

rit.

ONLY A DRUNKARD.—Concluded.

a tempo.

pass	him	not	by;	Ah, leave him not there To suf - fer and
fell	on	the	snow;	Take him to his mother, She will bless you I
on -	ly	re -	lief;	She clings to her dar - ling Tho' he causeth her
fall	in	the	snow;	The grief of such mothers God on - ly can

a tempo.

die, Look	on the poor fel-low and pass	him not by. . . .
know, Tho' 'twas on-ly	a drunk-ard that fell	on the snow. . .
grief, And tears for her child seem her	on -	ly re - lief. . . .
know, He	pit- ies these drunkards that fall	(*Omit.*) . . . . . .

rit.

ending for last verse.

in the snow. . . . .

cresc. *dim.*

No. 11.   THE WEDDING GARMENT.

L. E. J.   L. E. JONES.

1. Have you heard the in - vi - ta - tion, To the
2. Are you read - y for His com - ing, Be it
3. Will His smile to you be giv - en, And His
4. Put ye on what He has giv - en Bless - ed

mar- riage of the Son; Have you on the wedding gar - ment,
morn - ing, noon or night, Will your rai - ment bear in - spec - tion,
words bring joy for aye, Or will He look once up - on you,
robe of righteous-ness, Then re - joice at His ap - pear - ing,

Chorus.

That the King pro - vides each one?
And be pleas - ing in His sight?
And for - ev - er turn a - way?   } Have you on the wedding
For He comes your soul to bless.

gar - ment! Spot-less robe of pur - i - ty, Have you

on the wedding gar - ment, That the King de - lights to see?

No. 12. SOMETIME, SOMEWHERE.

CHARLIE D. TILLMAN.

1. Un-an-swered yet? The pray'r your lips have plead - ed In ag - o -
2. Un-an-swered yet? Tho' when you first pre- sent - ed This one pe -
3. Un-an-swered yet? Nay, do not say un- grant - ed; Perhaps your
4. Un-an-swered yet? Faith can-not be un - an-swered; Her feet were

ny of heart these many years? Does faith be - gin to fail, is hope de -
ti - tion at the Father's throne, It seemed you could not wait the time of
part is not yet whol-ly done; The work be-gan when first your pray'r was
firm - ly plant-ed on the Rock; A- mid the wild-est storms she stands un-

part - ing, And think you all in vain those fall- ing tears? Say not the
ask - ing. So ur-gent was your heart to make it known. Tho' years have
ut - tered, And God will fin - ish what He has be - gun. If you will
daunt - ed, Nor quails be - fore the loud- est thun- der shock. She knows Om-

Father hath not heard your pray'r; You shall have your desire sometime, some -
passed since then, do not de - spair; The Load will answer you sometime, some -
keep the in-cense burning there, His glo- ry you shall see, sometime, some -
nip-otence has heard her pray'r, And cries, "It shall be done," sometime, some -

rit . . . . *ad lib.*

where, You shall have your de - sire, some-time, some - where.
where, The Lord will an - swer you some-time, some - where.
where, His glo - ry you shall see, some-time, some - where.
where, and cries, "It shall be done," some-time, some - where.

2

No. 13. MARCHING TO VICTORY.

Rev. G. A. Le Clere.   O. E. Mattox.

1. March-ing a - long in glorious tri-umph in the arm - y of the Lord,
2. Onward we're marching fight-ing sin on ev-'ry bat-tle-field of life,
3. Then in the res- ur- rec-tion morning when the earth gives up its dead,

On our ban - ner is inscribed in gold, His ev - er - last - ing word;
Foes with - in and foes with-out, con-tend-ing with us in the strife;
We shall march in glo-rious triumph, with our ev - er liv - ing head;

Bless-ed as - sur- ance that He gives us as He sends us on our way;
Cour-age my broth- er, do not fal - ter, it is Sa - tan we're to fight;
Then will our Cap-tain be our Judge who knew our mor - al worth be-fore;

CHORUS.

"Ye shall conquer, I'll be with you in the fray."
Je - sus is our Captain, conquer in His might. } We are marching on in
We will wave the Palm of Vic-t'ry ev - er-more.

triumph in the arm - y of the Lord, Courage brother, do not fal-ter by the way, For our Cap-tain gone be-fore bids us nev - er be dismay'd,

He as - sures us vic - t'ry shall not be de - layed . . . . .

not be delayed.

No. 14. I CAN I WILL.

1. Re - fin - ing fire, go thro' my heart, Re - fin - ing fire, go thro' my heart,
2. Scat-ter thy life thro' ev - 'ry part, Scat-ter thy life thro' ev - 'ry part,
3. O that it now from heav'n might fall, O that it now from heav'n might fall,
4. Come, Ho-ly Ghost, for thee I call, Come, Ho - ly Ghost, for thee I call,

Сно. No. 1. I can, I will I do be-lieve, I can, I will, I do be-lieve,
Сно. No. 2. I'm kneel-ing at the mer - cy seat, I'm kneel-ing at the mer - cy seat,

Re - fin - ing fire, go thro' my heart, Il - lu - mi - nate my soul.
Scat - ter thy life thro' ev - 'ry part, And sanc - ti - fy the whole.
O that it now from heav'n might fall, And all my sins con - sume.
Come, Ho - ly Ghost, for thee I call, Spir - it of burn - ing, come.

I can, I will, I do be - lieve, That Je - sus saves me now.
I'm kneel-ing at the mer - cy seat, Where Je - sus an - swers pray'r.

No. 15. BRIGHTER AND BRIGHTER.

Dedicated to R. F. KILGORE.

CHARLIE D. TILLMAN.

1. The light of the word shines bright-er and bright-er, As
2. The wealth of this world seems poor-er and poor-er, As
3. My wait-ing on Je-sus is dear-er and dear-er, As
4. My joy in my Sav-iour is grow-ing and grow-ing, And

wid-er and wid-er God opens mine eyes; My tri-als and burdens seem
far-ther and farther it fades from my sight; The prize of my call-ing seems
long-er and long-er I lie on His breast; Without Him I'm nothing seems
stronger and stronger I trust in His Word; My peace like a riv-er is

light-er and light-er, And fair-er and fair-er the heav-en-ly prize.
sur-er and sur-er, As straighter and straighter I walk in the light.
clear-er and clear-er, And more and more sweetly in Je-sus I rest.
flowing and flow-ing, And hard-er and hard-er I lean on the Lord.

CHORUS.

This won - - der-ful sto - - ry I'm
This won-der-ful won-der-ful sto-ry I'm tell-ing, I'm

BRIGHTER AND BRIGHTER.—Concluded.

tell - - - ing and tell - - ing, And more . . . . and more
tell-ing of Je-sus I tell of His love, And more and more sweetly I

sweet - - ly I rest . . . . in His love, (in His love.)
rest in His love, And more and more sweetly I rest in His love.

No. 16. DOWN AT CALV'RYS FOUNTAIN.

L. E. J.

L. E. JONES.

1. I'm redeem'd and washed from sin, Down at Calv'rys fount - ain, There the cleansing
2. Joy I find be-yond compare, Down at Calv'rys fount - ain, Je - sus comes and
3. Bur-dens great are rolled a-way, Down at Calv'rys fount - ain, Strife with self all
4. Per - fect peace the Lord has giv'n, Down at Calv'rys fount - ain, Peace and rest like

Chorus.

tide comes in, Down at Cal-v'rys fount - ain.
meets me there, Down at Cal-v'rys fount - ain.
ceased for aye, Down at Cal-v'rys fount - ain.
that of heav'n, Down at Cal-v'rys fount - ain.

There is cleansing in the tide

As it flows from Calv'rys side, To my heart it is applied, Down at Calv'rys fountain.

No. 17. THE HEALED PINION.

J. R. B.

Jno. R. Bryant

Solo.

1. There's a song of a bro-ken pin - ion, Of a bird that loved to
2. There is ma-ny a life that's bro - ken, By the sin of drink or
3. 'Tis the life of the bro-ken heart - ed, That the Sav - ior doth gladly

sing, And the air was its do - min - ion, Till it
shame, With the Sav - ior they once were walk - ing, Till the
heal, To them of a con - trite spir - it, The

chanced to break its wing. And it lay on a bed of
tempter their faith o'er - came, In deep - est de - spair now
Lord will His love re - veal, Oh, come and your sins for -

THE HEALED PINION.—Concluded.

moss - es,   All help - less and faint with   pain,   But 'twas
wail - ing,   With no   one to soothe their   pain,   Go
giv - en,   The Sav - ior with you   will   reign,   He'll re -

heal'd and a - gain each morn-ing It would soar with its same sweet strain.
bring them to Him who heal - eth That they may be whole a - gain.
store   the joys de - part - ed, And will take you back a - gain.

CHORUS.

Then come,   to the Sav - ior, No matter how great thy sin............
Then come, yes come to the Savior, No matter how great, how great thy sin,

He can heal the bro - ken pin - ion Of those who would soar a - gain.

No. 18. DO NOT TRY, BUT TRUST.

MINNIE B. JOHNSON. JNO. R. BRYANT.

1. Noth-ing is gain'd by try-ing, Noth-ing from self can come,
2. Deeds that are good we're do-ing, Dai-ly the world to see,
3. Work-ing for Christ is pleas-ure, When done in His great name;

'Tis on the blood re-ly-ing, Trust-ing the Ho-ly One.
Lost ones to Christ we're wooing, Try-ing thus good to be.
Noth-ing we do could mer-it, Aught in His glo-rious fame.

'Tis not thy works that saves thee, For there- in man might boast,
Noth-ing in us is wor-thy, Weak creatures form'd of dust,
Sim-ply by faith re-ceiv-ing Him as the Christ—we must,

Sim-ply in Christ be-liev-ing, It is not Try, but Trust.
In Him's the work of sav-ing, Then do not Try, but Trust.
Then on His pow'r be-liev-ing, We will not Try, but Trust.

Chorus.

It is not Try, but Trust, It is not Try, but Trust,

DO NOT TRY, BUT TRUST.—Concluded.

Noth- ing of self is de-serv- iug, Then do not Try, but Trust.

No. 19. AT THE FOUNTAIN.

Old Melody.

1. Of Him who did sal - va- tion bring, I'm at the fountain drink-ing,
2. Ask but His grace and lo! 'tis giv'u, I'm at the fountain drink-ing,
3. Tho' sin and sor-row wound my soul, I'm at the fountain drink-iug,
4. Wher-e'er I am, where'er I move, I'm at the fountain drink-ing.
5. In - sa- tiate to this spring I fly, I'm at the fountain drink-ing,

I could for - ev - er think and sing, I'm on my jour- ney home.
Ask and He turns your hell to heav'n, I'm on my jour- ney home.
Je - sus, Thy balm will make me whole, I'm on my jour- ney home.
I meet the ob - ject of my love, I'm on my jour- ney home.
I drink and yet am ev - er dry, I'm on my jour- ney home.

Chorus.

Glo - ry to God, I'm at the fountain drinking, on my journey home.

No. 20. KEEP US IN THY FOLD.

GEO. W. LYON.   JNO. R. BRYANT.

1. Gen- tle Shepherd keeps us in Thy fold, With thy kind embrace, In this
2. Sav- iour, let Thy truth now light our way, Be a lamp so bright to dis -
3. Sav- iour 'neath the banner of Thy love, To each one re- peat, 'till a -

heav'nly place, Give to us that peace of mind un- told, And to
pel our night, Be a guide to us we hum-bly pray, And with-
gain we meet; Bath - ings from that sa - cred fount a - bove, 'Till a -

Refrain.

us im - part Thy heav'nly grace. Sav - - iour, gen- tle
hold us in Thy pow'rful might.
round Thy throne we stand complete. Sav-iour, gen-tle Sav - iour,

Sav - - iour. Let us ev- er in Thy fold a- bide, Nev - -
Saviour, gentle Saviour,   Nev-er let us

er, let us nev - - er, Wan-der from Thy blessed side.
leave Thee, nev- er let us leave, nor

No. 21. I ONLY KNOW IT REACHES ME.

MINNIE B. JOHNSON.

JNO. R. BRYANT.

1. I know not why God's wondrous grace, To all the world He of-fers free ;
2. I know not why such sav-ing faith As this could ev - er, ev - er be ;
3. I know not why the Spir-it comes A wit-ness in my soul to be ;
4. I know not why these gifts to man, Or what in man the Lord could see ;

Nor why His love shall nev-er cease, I on - ly know it reach-es me.
Bestowed on one of lit-tle worth, I on - ly know it reach-es me.
To wit-ness to the cleansing pow'r, I on - ly know it reach-es me.
To move Him seal, such boun teous grace, I on - ly know it reach-es me.

Chorus.

It reach - es me . . . . . . it reach - es me,
It reaches me   it reach-es me,

God's grace so wondrous reaches me, I know not why . . . it is so
I know not why

free (it is so free,) I on - ly know it reach-es me. (it reach-es me.)

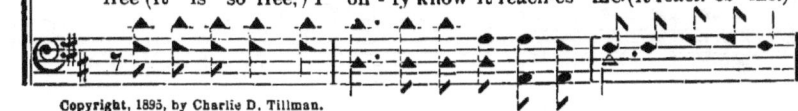

No. 22. O LET THE CURRENT IN.

L. E. J.

L. E. JONES.

1. My broth-er there's a foun-tain, That cleans-es from all sin,
2. The Sav-ior now is plead-ing, He died your soul to win,
3. The stream from Calv'ry's mountain Will pu-ri-fy with-in,

Then throw the heart's door o-pen, And let its cur-rent in.
He set the stream a flow-ing, O let its cur-rent in.
Give bless-ed rest and com-fort O let its cur-rent in.

Chorus.

O let the cur-rent in, 'Twill free your heart from sin,
Last Chorus.
I've let the cur-rent in, And I am freed from sin,

From Je-sus side 'tis flow-ing, O let the cur-rent in.
Oh! glo-ry Je-sus saves me, I've let the cur-rent in.

No. 23. BEAUTIFUL LIGHT OF THE CROSS.

Mrs. E. W. Chapman.   Jno. R. Bryant.

1. Dear Redeem - er let Thy Spir - it, Now our tho'ts of Thee in- dict,
2. Make us faith- ful in Thy vine - yard, Bringing ma - ny souls to Thee,
3. Help us Lord in ev - 'ry ef - fort, Grant us Thy sustain-ing grace,

Let the bless - ed cross of Cal - vary, Shine a-round us with its light.
That within the ark of Ref - uge, They may ev - er safe - ly be.
Let Thy glo - ry light our path - way, As we run the heav'nly race.

Chorus.

Thou beau - - - - - ti - ful Light of the cross, Now

Thou beau - ti - ful Light of the cross now shine, Now

shine with Thy heav-en- ly rays, A - round us with

shine with Thy heav'nly rays now shine A - round us with glo-rious

glo - rious light,

light now shine, Shine, on O, beau - ti - ful Light of the cross.

No. 24. PAPA'S LATE TRAIN.

In a revival meeting, a railroad engineer arose and said, " Yesterday morning my little girl of four was taken suddenly ill after I had gone out on my regular run to be back at seven to-night. I pulled in one hour late, hurried home and found she had been dead five minutes. Her last words were, " Mamma ! Papa's train is too late for me to kiss him good-bye." With tearful eyes he said, " You wonder why I am here and my little one at home a corpse; It is that I may get help."

Mrs. GERTIE JONES.   CHARLIE D. TILLMAN.

1. A lit- tle one toss'd on a bed of pain, At the close of a
2. "His train was due at sev- en, mamma, And now it is
3. Swift o - ver the rails thro' the gloom of the night, An en - gine came
4. Death's train swiftly bore her sweet spir- it a- way, Ere her pa - pa's late
5. Oh! fathers, have you in that beau-ti- ful land, Some treasured and in -

sad, sad day, The an - gel of death was hov - 'ring near To
near- ly eight, I want- ed to kiss my pa- pa goodbye, I'm a -
thund'ring down, An hour behind as the wheels stood still, 'Mid the
train mov'd in ; No un- ion now of that heav'n - ly land, With
no-cent one, Who, safe from the sorrows and cares of life, Is

bear her sweet spir - it a - way. But with dim eyes fix'd on the
fraid he will be too late." Of death's i - cy touch she
glim-mer - ing lights of the town : The en - gi-neer rushed home with a
this one of troub- le and sin Con - nec - tion lost by an
wait- ing for pa - pa to come? Can it be that this earth is

old clock nigh, She count-ed the moments as they went by, And with
had no fear, Her kind, lov-ing Sav - iour seem-ed so near ; Her
trou - ble deep, And knelt by the cot, but too stricken to weep, He had
hour's de- lay, The ac - cept-ed time had pass-ed a-way ; Ah,
all your goal, That you'll tri- fle with God and your own soul, And

plain- tive, fee- ble and trem - bling cry, said, "Pa- pa will be too
tho'ts were all for her pa - pa dear, Oh, would he be too
miss'd the kiss of his darling's last sleep, For pa - pa had come too
sad the one who is left to say, "I came too late, too
be as years of e - ter - ni - ty roll, For-ev - er and ev - er too

ad lib . . . .

late! Oh, pa-pa will be too late, Oh, pa-pa will be too late!"
late? Oh, would he be too late, Oh, would he be too late?
late, For pa-pa had come too late, Yes pa-pa had come too late.
late, I came too late, too late, I came too late, too late."
late? For-ev-er and ev-er too late, For-ev-er and ev-er too late?

No. 25.   O HOW I LOVE HIM!

J. R. B.   J. R. BRYANT.

1. I have found a precious Friend, O how I love Him! He will serve me
2. He is ev-'ry thing to me, O how I love Him! My sal-va-tion
3. At His feet I hum-bly fall, O how I love Him! Je-sus is my

to the end, O how I love Him! To my needs He gives re-lief, To my
sure is He, O how I love Him! Je-sus, Je-sus is His name, For my
all in all, O how I love Him! A-do-ra-tion now I bring, To my

doubts He gives be-lief, From my heart dispels all grief, O how I love Him!
sins He bore the shame, He unchanging will remain, O how I love Him!
Saviour, Priest and King, Now and ev-er will I sing. O how I love Him!

No. 26. What Will it Matter By and By?

J. R. B.

Jno. R. Bryant.

1. What will it mat-ter by and by, Wheth-er my path be-
2. What will it mat-ter by and by, Wheth-er my bur-den
3. What will it mat-ter by and by, Wheth-er to me much
4. What will it mat-ter by and by, Wheth-er with friends, my

low was bright? Whether 'twas stones within the way, Or strewn with
here was light? Whether with cares of life bow'd down, Or blest with
good was sent? Wheth-er in tri-al sore dis-may, Or in re-
life was spent? Whether in for-eign lands my call, Wheth-er in

ro-ses bright and gay, What will it mat-ter by and by?
joys of bright re-nown, What will it mat-ter by and by?
joic-ing ev-'ry day, What will it mat-ter by and by?
heath-en hands I fall, What will it mat-ter by and by?

Refrain.

What will it mat-ter? What will it matter? What will it matter by and by?

3

No. 27. DIAMONDS IN THE ROUGH.

CHARLIE D. TILLMAN.

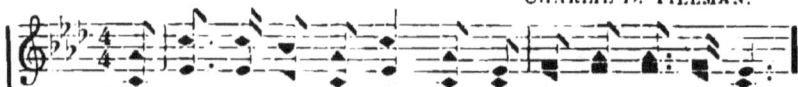

1. Ah, ma - ny hearts are ach - ing; We find them ev - 'ry-where,
2. One day, my pre-cious com - rade, You, too, were lost in sin :
3. So let us keep it burn - ing. The lamp of ho - ly love,

Whose cups are filled with sor - row, Whose homes are filled with care ;
But oth - ers sought your res - cue, And Je - sus took you in ;
To ev - 'ry per - se - cu - tor, Point out the way a - bove ;

When mis-for - tune o - ver-takes them, The world gives them a cuff,
So, when you're tried and tempt-ed, By the scof-fer's keen re - buff,
The pre-cious blood of Je - sus Was shed for that poor tough,

Or sends them to per - di - tion, Those dia-monds in the rough.
Don't turn a - way in an - ger, He's a dia-mond in the rough.
Oh, let us tell him of it, That dia-mond in the rough.

DIAMONDS IN THE ROUGH.—Concluded.

The day will soon be o-ver, In which to work and win,

Ma-ny a gem lies hid-den Be-neath the dross of sin,

Oh, let us dig and find them! God's pow-er is e-nough

To pol-ish in-to beau-ty Those dia-monds in the rough.

No. 28. When I Get to the End of the Way.

* * *

CHARLIE D. TILLMAN.

1. The sands have been washed in the footprints Of the stranger on
2. There are so many hills to climb upward, I often am
3. He loves me too well to forsake me Or give me one
4. When the last feeble step has been taken And the gates of that

D.C.—And the toils of the road will seem nothing, When I get to the
Last.—Then the toils of the road will seem nothing, When I get to the

Gal - i - lee's shore, And the voice that subdued the rough billows,
long - ing for rest. But He who appoints me my pathway,
tri - al too much, All His people have been dearly purchased,
cit - y appear And the beautiful songs of the angels

end of the way, And the toils of the road will seem nothing,
end of the way, Then the toils of the road will seem nothing,

FINE.

Will be heard in Ju-de-a no more. But the path of that
Knows just what is needful and best. I know in His
And sa-tan can never claim such. By and by I shall
Float out on my list-en-ing ear. When all that now seems

When I get to the end of the way.
When I get to the end of the way.

D.C.

lone Gal - i - lee - an With joy I will fol-low to-day.
word He hath promised That my strength "it shall be as my day."
see Him and praise Him, In the cit - y of un-end-ing day.
so mys-te - ri-ous Will be bright and as clear as the day.

No. 29. SWEEPING THROUGH THE GATES.

Arr. by J. L. M.

J. L. MOORE. By per.

1. I am now a child of God, I've been wash'd in Je-sus' blood, I am
2. Oh, the bless-ed Lord of light Now up-holds me by His might, And His
3. I am sweep-ing thro' the gate, Where the bless-ed for me wait, Where the
4. Burst are all my pris-on bars, And I soar be-yond the stars, To my

watching and I'm longing while I wait; Soon on wings of love I'll fly, To a
arms en-fold and com-fort while I wait; I am lean-ing on His breast; Oh, the
wea-ry work-ers rest for-ev-er-more; Where the strife of earth is done, And the
Fa-ther's house, the bright and blest estate; Lo! the morn e-ter-nal breaks, And the

D.S. *In the blood of Calv'ry's Lamb, Wash'd from*

home be-yond the sky, To my wel-come, as I'm sweeping thro' the
sweet-ness of this rest! Hal-le-lu-jah! I am sweeping thro' the
crown of life is won, Oh, the glo-ry of that cit-y just be-
song im-mor-tal wakes, Wash'd in Je-sus' blood, I'm sweeping thro' the

ev-'ry stain I am, Hal-le-lu-jah! I am sweep-ing thro' the

FINE. CHORUS.

gates.
gates.
fore!
gates.   Sweep - - - ing thro' the gates,
gates.   Sweeping thro' the gates; Yes, I'm sweeping thro' the gates;

gates.

D.S.

Sweep - - - ing thro' the gates.
Sweep-ing thro' the gates; Yes, I'm sweep-ing thro' the gates.

No. 30. TOILING NOW, RESTING THEN.

Words and Music by JNO. R. BRYANT.

1. I have work e - nough to do, In a field that's ev - er new, While I'm
2. There's a sto - ry to re - peat That is ev - er new and sweet, While I'm
3. Now I walk the liv - ing way, I have Je - sus for my stay, While I'm
4. I'll have Je - sus by my side, When I cross the storm-y tide, When done

toil - ing in the vine-yard of the Lord. I can nev - er wea - ry grow, For His
toil - ing in the vine-yard of the Lord. 'T is of Je - sus and His love, Sung by
toil - ing in the vine-yard of the Lord. In this bless-ed gos-pel light, Love my
toil - ing in the vine-yard of the Lord. There His glo - ry I shall see, In His

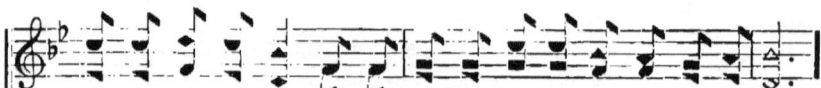

love I on - ly know, While I'm toil - ing in the vine-yard of the Lord.
flam - ing tongues a - bove, While I 'm toil - ing in the vine - yard of the Lord.
Sav - iour and the right, While I 'm toil - ing in the vine - yard of the Lord.
like - ness I shall be, When done toil - ing in the vine - yard of the Lord.

CHORUS.

1, 2, 3. Toil - ing, toil - ing, toil-ing for the Mas-ter, Ev -'ry day, Him o - bey. Should the
4. Rest - ing, rest - ing, resting with the Mas-ter, While the song Rolls a - long, Oh, the

way seem rough and long, I can cheer it with a song, While I'm toiling in the vineyard of the Lord.
joys shall never cease. For His glory shall increase, While I'm resting in the presence of the Lord.

No. 31. SINCE TO MY HEART JESUS CAME.

L. E. J.   L. E. JONES.

1. I have been saved from the pow'r of sin; Since to my
2. Rest I have found from the cares of life, Since to my
3. Things of this world I de - sire no more, Since to my
4. I am led safe - ly from day to day, Since to my

heart Je-sus came, Washed at the fount-ain made white and clean,
heart Je-sus came, Par - don and peace, af - ter wea - ry strife,
heart Je-sus came, Bur- dens are lift - ed that once I bore;
heart Je-sus came, Glad - ly I walk in the nar - row way,

Chorus.

Since to my heart Je - sus came. Earth is so fair, and the
sky is so bright, Troub-les are scat-tered and toil seems so light
Safe-ly I'm kept through His love and His might, Since to my heart Je-sus came.

No. 32. THERE'S WORK TO DO.

GEO. W. LYON.   JNO. R. BRYANT.

1. Why stand ye i - dle all the day? There's something you can do;
2. Don't say you are too young or old, Un - fit and bus - y too,
3. Be up and do - ing for the Lord, And to His cause be true,

The field is wide, the lab'rers scarce, And there is work for you.
There is no need of such ex-cuse, And it is naught to you.
He waits with o - pen hands to bless, For all the work you do.

Chorus.

There's work, . . . yes work, ... There's work e-nough for you,
There's work for you, yes work to do,

In the high-ways, in the by-ways, You'll ev-er find work to do.

No. 33. THERE IS POWER IN THE BLOOD.

L. E. J.   L. E. JONES.

1. There's an o - pen fountain at the cross, I have plunged beneath its flow,
2. I have gained a bless- ed vic - to- ry; Since the cleansing tide came in,
3. I have found a joy in Je-sus' love, Like a taste of heav'nly rest,

Since the crimson cur-rent o'er me rolled, I am washed as white as snow.
With my Saviour walk-ing by my side I have conquered self and sin.
I am lean - ing hard the whole day long On His kind and shelt'ring breast.

Chorus.

There is won - drous pow'r in the Sav - iour's blood,
wondrous pow'r, wondrous pow'r in the blood, in the blood.

To my heart ap-plied 'Tis a pre-cious heal - ing flood.
To my heart now ap-plied

No. 34. In the Christian's Home in Glory.

JOHN 11: 2.

SAMUEL YOUNG HARMER, 1856.   WM. McDONALD, 1856.

1. In the Christian's home in glo - ry There re-mains a land of rest,
2. Pain and sick-ness ne'er shall en - ter, Grief nor woe my lot shall share,
3. Sing. O sing, ye heirs of glo - ry, Shout your tri - umph as you go;

There my Sav-iour's gone be - fore me, To ful - fill my soul's re-quest.
But in that ce - les - tial cen - ter I a crown of life shall wear.
Zi - on's gate will o - pen for you, You shall find an entrance thro'.

Chorus.

{ There is rest for the wea - ry, There is rest for the wea - ry,
{ On the oth - er side of Jor - dan, In the sweet fields of E - den.

There is rest for the wea - ry, There is rest for you, }
Where the tree of life is blooming, There is rest for you. {

No. 35. HE MAKETH THE STORM A CALM.

IDA L. REED. JNO. R. BRYANT.

1. He mak-eth the storm a calm, The winds there-of are still,
2. He calm-eth the storm-tossed soul, He bids its doubtings cease,
3. He mak-eth the storm a calm, He stilleth the troubled sea,

He speak-eth and they are hush'd, All things o-bey His will.
Tho' wild-ly the bil-lows roll His word brings to thee peace.
No tem-pest can us o'er-whelm, Our ref-uge He will be.

Refrain.

He calm-eth the troub-led heart, When waves of sor-row rise,

He bid-deth our griefs de-part, He dries our tear-ful eyes.

FANNY J. CROSBY.   W. H. DOANE.

1. There's a cit - y that looks o'er the val-ley of death, And its glo-ries can
2. There the King, our Redeemer, the Lord whom we love, All the faithful with
3. Ev - ery soul we have led to the foot of the cross, Ev-'ry lamb we have

nev - er be told; There the sun nev- er sets, and the leaves never fade,
rap- ture be-hold; There the righteous for-ev - er shall shine as the stars,
brought to the fold, Shall be kept as bright jew- els our crowns to a- dorn,

D.S.—And the eyes of the faith- ful our Sav - iour behold,

In that beau-ti- ful cit - y of Gold. ⎫ There the sun,   nev - er
In that beau-ti- ful cit - y of Gold. ⎬
In that beau-ti- ful cit - y of Gold. ⎭ there the sun,

FINE.

In that beau-ti- ful cit - y of Gold.

D.S.

sets,   and the leaves   nev - er fade;
nev - er sets,   and the leaves

SAFE WITHIN THE VAIL.

J. M. EVANS.

1. "Land a - head! its fruits are waving O'er the hills of fadeless green:
2. On-ward, bark! the cape I'm rounding; See the bless - ed wave their hands;
3. There, let go the anchor, rid-ing On this calm and sil-v'ry bay;
4. Now we're safe from all tempta-tion; All the storms of life are past;

And the liv - ing wa-ters lav-ing Shores where heav'nly forms are seen.
Hear the harps of God resounding, From the bright im-mor-tal bands.
Seaward fast the tide is glid-ing, Shores in sun-light glide a - way.
Praise the Rock of our sal- va-tion, We are safe at home at last.

Chorus.

Rocks and storms I'll fear no more When on that e - ter-nal shore;

Drop the an- chor! Furl the sail! I am safe with- in the vail.

No. 38.

1 O happy day, that fixed my choice
On Thee, my Saviour and my God!
Well may this glowing heart rejoice,
And tell its raptures all abroad.

CHO.—Happy day, etc.

2 O happy bond, that seals my vows,
To Him who merits all my love;
Let cheerful anthems fill His house,
While to that sacred shrine I move.

3 'Tis done, the great transaction's done;
I am my Lord's, and He is mine;
He drew me, and I followed on,
Charmed to confess the voice divine

MINNIE B. JOHNSON.   JNO. R. BRYANT.

1. To the cross, Christian soldiers, Press the bat-tle for the Lord,
2. To the cross, Christian soldiers, Hear the bless-ed Sav-iour's voice,
3. To the cross, Christian soldiers, To the con-flict we must go,

To   the   cross!. . . . .   to   the   cross!. . . . . .
To   the   cross!. . . . . .   to   the   cross!. . . . . .
With   the   cross, ...   with   the   cross, ...

               we   will fly,   live   or   die.

For our sword, and   our ar-mour We   will take our Saviour's word,
"Leave the world far   be-hind thee Make me   now thine on-ly choice,"
In His name press   the bat-tle, Till   we con-quer ev-'ry foe,

To   the   cross, ... we'll haste a - way.
To   the   cross, ... oh haste   a - way.
At   the   cross, ... we'll ev - er   stay.

               To the cross we'll haste   a - way, (we'll haste a-way.)
               To the cross oh haste   a - way, (oh haste a - way.)
               At the cross we'll ev - er   stay, (we'll ev-er stay.)

TO THE CROSS.—Concluded.

Refrain.

To the cross,..... we'll haste a - way,

To the cross, we'll haste a - way,

Chris-tian sol - - diers don't de - lay,

Chris-tian sol-diers don't de - lay,

Live or die in its glo - ry we will here for ev - er stay,

At the cross,..... yes, at the cross.

At the cross, yes, at the cross.

No. 40.   WILL YOU COME JUST NOW?

Minnie B. Johnson.   Jno. R. Bryant.

1. Hear the bless - ed   in - vi - ta - tion, Will   you come just now?
2. Hear the voice of   Je - sus call - ing Will   you come just now?
3. Hear the Spir - it's   in - ter - ced - ing, Will   you come just now?

To the wa - ters   of   sal - va - tion, Will   you come just now?
On your ear the   ac - cents fall - ing Will   you come just now?
And the Bride with thee   is   plead - ing Will   you come just now?

Liv - ing streams for - ev - er   flow, Where the tree   of   life doth grow,
Has - ten   sin - ner to the brink, Of   the sav - ing wa - ter drink,
It   is   bid - den him that hear, Sound the mes - sage sweet and clear,

Of   its   vir - tues   all   may know, Will   you   come just now?
Ere   your sun   in wrath shall sink, Will   you   come just now?
He   that is   a - thirst draw near, Will   you   come just now?

WILL YOU COME JUST NOW? Concluded.

REFRAIN.

O will you come, ... O will you come, ...
O will you come, O will you come,

To the fount-ain full and free, It is flow-ing now for thee,

O will you come, ... O will you come .....
O will you come, O will you come

To the fount-ain will you come just now? ....
Will you come just now?

No. 41.   A LITTLE TALK WITH JESUS.

"And behold there talked with Him two men." Luke ix: 30.

ANON.   Arranged.

1. While fight - ing for my Sav - iour here, The dev - il tries me hard; He
2. Tho' dark the night, and clouds look black, And stormy o - ver - head, And
3. When those who once were dear - est friends Be - gin to per - se - cute, And
4. And thus, by fre - quent lit - tle talks I gain the vic - to - ry; And

us - es all His might - y pow'r, My pro - gress to re - tard; He's
trials of al - most ev - 'ry kind A - cross my path are spread; How
more who once pro - fessed to love, Have dis - tant grown, and mute, I
march a - long with cheer - ful song, En - joy - ing lib - er - ty; With

up to ev - 'ry move, And yet through all I prove, A lit - tle talk with
soon I con - quer all, As to the Lord I call, A lit - tle talk with
tell Him all my grief, He quick - ly sends re - lief, A lit - tle talk with
Je - sus as my Friend, I'll prove un - til the end, A lit - tle talk with

D.S. *trials of ev - 'ry kind, Praise God, I al - ways find, A lit - tle talk with*

CHORUS.

Je - sus makes it right, all right. A lit - tle talk with Je - sus makes it

Je - sus makes it right, all right.

D.S.

right, all right, A lit - tle talk with Je - sus makes it right, all right. In

No. 42. MOVING TOWARD THE CITY.

" For here have we no continuing city, but seek for one to come."—HEB. 13: 14.

Mrs. E. W. CHAPMAN.　　　　　　　　　　　J. H. TENNEY.

1. We are mov-ing toward the Cit - y;　Far-ther on　we　pitch our tents ;
2. We are mov-ing toward the Cit - y,—Rest-ing not　in　fer - tile plains ;
3. We are mov-ing toward the Cit - y,　In　the path the　ran-somed trod ;

As　we climb the green-clad highlands, Glo- ry shines on　us　from thence.
Ev - 'ry day's march brings us near-er Where the King in　glo- ry　reigns.
Tent- ing near - er,　near-er,　near - er　To　the pal - ace of　our God.

Chorus.

We　　　　　　　are　　mov - - ing,　　With the
We are mov-ing, With the Saviour for our guide, We are mov- ing,

Sav-iour for　our guide;　　　　　　　We　　　　　are
for our guide; We are tenting, Nearer to fair Canaan's

tent - - ing,　Near - er　to　　　fair　Ca - naan's side.
side　we　are tent- ing, Near - er,　near- er　to

No. 43. ARE YOU WATCHING?

EMILY C. PEARSON. HAMP. H. SEWELL by per.

1. Are you watch-ing for the glo - ry Of the com- ing of the Lord,
2. It will be at time ap-point-ed, Tho' we may not know the day,
3. One is tak - en at the midnight In his peace-ful hour of rest,

As fore- told by seers and prophets, And His own oft-spok- en word;
He would find us oc - cu - py-ing, When He calls His own a - way;
Borne a - way with oth- ers ransomed, To the gath'ring of the blest;

Are you wait-ing while He tar - ries, Tho' He com - eth not as yet,
One is tak - en from His field-work, And the oth - er toil- er left,
Be then watching for the glo - ry, Of the com - ing of the King,

He hath made a sure appointment, And the ver - y time is set.
Who had nev - er sought the Sav-iour, Of sal - va - tion he's be - reft.
As fore- told by seers and prophets, When His loved ones He will bring.

ARE YOU WATCHING?—Concluded.

Refrain.

Then be watch - ing, ... oh be wait - ing, ...
watching, watching, waiting, watching, wait- ing, wait- ing,

Will you re - sist His own oft-spok - en word,
re-sist it not,

Then be watch - ing, ... oh be wait - ing, ...
watching, watching, waiting, watching, waiting, waiting,

Yes watch - ing for the com - ing of the Lord.

No. 44. THE LAST CHANCE.

Rev. Geo. A. LeClere.

O. E. Mattox.

1. Do you hear the voice of God As He call-eth now to thee:
2. Ma-ny times that voice has come, Call-ing thee from paths of sin;
3. Now's the time to let Him in, While He calls to thee to-day;
4. Now I see my life's mis-take, And I'm com-ing to the Lord,

Hear Him speak in tenderest tones, As He calls to mer-cy free;
Knock-ing at the heart's-door loud, Plead-ing that you let Him in;
O - pen wide the heart's-door now, E're He turns from thee a - way:
It is "now's the time" to come, So I read His bless-ed word:

Oft He calls thee to His breast, And He of - fers to thy soul
Yet you've turned Him from your heart, By your sin you've barred the door,
All the lost souls now that die, In the land of deep de-spair,
Now I come my heart to cast At the bless-ed Sav-iour's feet,

Wea - ry with its bur - den, rest sweet rest.
You have caused the Spir - it to de - part.
Let their last chance to be saved pass by.
For I fear this chance will be the last.

THE LAST CHANCE.—Concluded.

Chorus.

There is a last chance for sal - va - tion,
There is a last chance for sal - va - tion,

Cho. for last verse.
Lord, I am com - - ing yes I'm com - ing,
Lord, I am com - ing, yes I am com-ing,

Do you not hear Him ten - der - ly call - ing—
Do you not hear Him tender-ly call-ing.

Down at Thy feet I pa - tient - ly lin - ger,
Down at Thy feet I patient-ly lin- ger,

Ur - gent - ly call - ing, long He has wait - ed,
Urgent-ly call-ing long He has wait-ed,

Je - sus re - ceive me, cleanse and re - lieve me,
Je-sus re-ceive me, cleanse and relieve me,

Turn, O sin - ner ere it is too late.
it is too late.

I am com - ing now with - out de - lay,
with-out de - lay.

No. 45. SAUL'S JOURNEY TO DAMASCUS.

J. A. B. JAMES A. BUCHANAN.

Modera

1. When the peo - ple of God were wor- ship-ing, In Da-mas - cus not
2. Then He said who art thou, Lord I pray, And what wilt thou now
3. Then straightway did the chief of sin - ners go To re-ceive God's own
4. Guilt - y sin - ner, the Lord is call - ing thee, Will you hear while the

far o'er the way; From the blood-thirsty throng at Je - ru - sa - lem
have me to do; Then the Lord said to him, a - rise, I say,
word thro' His Son Bless- ed word which is life to the sin - sick soul,
voice still doth cry, Will you take His sal - va - tion so great and free.

Chorus.

Journeyed Saul to bring them a- way. } As he journeyed he heard a voice
'T will be told thee what thou must do. }
From the cross to the bright, golden crown. } Cho.—4th. verse.
While e - ter-ni-ties drawing so nigh. } Will you hear while the voice is calling

say. Saul, oh Saul, why per - se - cu - test me: I am the
now, oh sin - ners, oh wilt thou come to me; I am thy

Lord of heav'n and earth, I am Je - sus who died on the tree.
light and sav - ing pow'r, I am Je - sus who died on the tree.

No. 46. I'M WAITING FOR JESUS TO COME.

" Having a desire to depart and to be be with Christ, which is far better."—
PHIL. 1 : 23.

JOHN.

J. G. F.

1. I'm wait-ing for Je-sus to wel-come me home, Glad when my
2. My Je-sus, I long for a sight of Thy face, Bright-er by
3. I want to be faith-ful while tar-ry-ing here, Wish-ing to

jour-ney is run; There sor-row and troub-le shall nev-er be known.
far than the sun; I'd fly to Thy bos-om and there be at rest,
hear Thy "well done;" I know that my Sav-iour will short-ly ap-pear,

Chorus.

I'm wait-ing for Je-sus to come. ⎫
I'm wait-ing for Je-sus to come. ⎬   I'm wait-ing,   just
I'm wait-ing for Je-sus to come. ⎭   I'm wait-ing,

wait-ing, I'm wait-ing for Je-sus to come, I'm wait-ing   just
just wait-ing,   I'm wait-ing,

wait-ing,   I'm wait-ing for Je-sus to come.
just wait-ing,

No. 47.   TRUST ON.

Anon.   HAMP. H. SEWELL, by per.

1. Trust on, trust on be - liev - er, Tho' long the con - flict be,
2. Trust on, trust on, thy fail - ings May bow thee to the dust.
3. Trust on, the dan- ger press - es, Temp - ta - tion strong is near,
4. O Christ is strong to save us, He is a faith- ful friend,

Thou yet shalt prove vic - to - rious, Thy God shall fight for thee.
But in thy deep - est sor - row, O give not up thy trust.
Yet o'er life's dan- g'rous rap - ids, He shall thy pas- sage steer.
Trust on, trust on be - liev - er, O trust Him to the end.

Refrain.

Trust on, trust on Tho' dark the night and drear,
trust on, trust on,

Trust on . . . . The morn- ing dawn is near.
trust on, trust on, trust on,

No. 48. BLESSED ASSURANCE.

"He is faithful that hath promised."—Heb. 10 : 23.

F. J. Crosby.   Mrs. Jos. F. Knapp.

1. Bless-ed as-sur-ance, Je-sus is mine! Oh what a fore-taste of
2. Per-fect sub-mis-sion, per-fect de-light, Vis-ions of rap-ture now
3. Per-fect sub-mis-sion, all is at rest, I in my Sav-iour am

glo-ry di-vine! Heir of sal-va-tion, purchased of God, Born of His
burst on my sight, An-gels de-scending, bring from above, Ech-oes of
hap-py and blest, Watching and waiting, looking a-bove, Filled with His

Chorus.

Spir-it, washed in His blood. }
mer-cy, whis-pers of love.   } This is my sto-ry, this is my
good-ness, lost in His love.   }

song, Prais-ing my Sav-iour all the day long; This is my

sto-ry, this is my song, Prais-ing my Saviour all the day long.

WHITER THAN SNOW.

D. S. WARNER. B. E. WARREN.

Allegro.

1. Re-joice lit-tle ones in the prom-ise di-vine, The Sav-iour has
2. Look up-ward to Je-sus, He's might-y to save; His love like the
3. A-dieu to this world, if you'd fol-low the Lord, For none but the
4. We go not to heav-en, sal-va-tion to know, But Je-sus came
5. Oh, do not dis-hon-or the name of our King, To think that you

willed that His glo-ry be thine; Then walk in white rai-ment with
o-cean, oh, sink in its wave; Here wash in the blood of the
pure are re-ceived by His word; Un-spot-ted from sin and made
down to make whit-er than snow; He'll wait not death's com-ing as-
can-not be free from all sin: He died to re-deem you, His

Him here be-low, The sheep of His fold must be whit-er than snow.
cru-ci-fied one, And shout His sal-va-tion in heav-en be-gun.
per-fect in love, As pure in this world as in heav-en a-bove.
sist-ance to lend, But save you just now, and to worlds with-out end.
prom-ise is sure, He'll wash you and keep you e-ter-nal-ly pure.

Chorus.

Whit - - - er than snow . . . .
Whit - er, dear Sav - iour, I'm whit - er than snow,

Whit - - er than snow, ... Whit - - er than

Glo - ry to Je - sus! my heart is a - glow, Whit-er, dear Sav-iour, I'm

snow .... Whit - - - er than snow .....

whit - er than snow. Kept by His pow - er, I'm whit - er than snow.

No. 50.   BLEST BE THE TIE.

JOHN FAWCETT.   GEO. NAEGELI.

1. Blest be   the   tie   that binds Our hearts in Chris - tian love; The
2. Be - fore   our Father's throne, We pour our ar - dent pray'rs; Our
3. When we   a - sun - der part. It gives us in - ward pain; But

fel - low - ship of kin - dred minds Is like   to   that a - bove.
fears, our   hopes, our aims are one, Our com - forts and our cares.
we   shall still   be joined in heart, And hope to   meet a - gain.

No. 51.   WAIT ON THE LORD.

Ps. 37 : 34.

IDA L. REED.   W. A. OGDEN.

Slow and strong.

1. Wait on the Lord, thy   Sav-iour and King, Trust in His word His
2. Wait on the Lord, and   bring Him thy care, Kneel at His throne find
3. Wait on the Lord, for - get not His way, He will re-ward thy

praise ev - er sing; Wait on the Lord and keep thou His way,
ref - uge in prayer, Tell Him thy woes, this Sav-iour of thine,
work ev-ery day, Trust thou,and wait tho' bless-ings be few,

D.S.—Wait on the Lord, be patient and true,

FINE. Chorus.

Pray Him to guard thy foot-steps to-day.
Free - ly o'er flows His pit - y di-vine. } Wait on the Lord thy
Ev - er He'll aid His fol - low - ers true.

He will a Fa-ther be un - to you.

D.S.

Sav - iour and King, Trust in His word, His praise ev - er sing;

By per of W. A. Ogden.

No. 52.   HALLELUJA!·

C. D. T.   Melody furnished by the Salvation Army.
Arr. by CHARLIE D. TILLMAN.

1. I now have the Spirit that setteth me free, Hal - le - lu - ja!
2. No long-er I'm doubting His power to save,
3. So glad I can trust Him I cannot but shout,
4. My Saviour is with me each day in the year, Hal-le, hal-le - lu - ja!

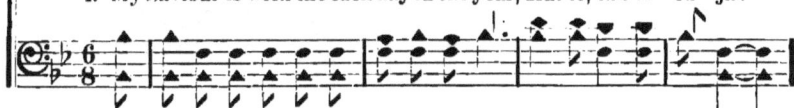

My Sav - iour's presence a - bideth with me, Hal - le - lu - ja!
The world - ly pleasures no long-er I crave,
The in-bred cor-ruption is all tak-en out,
A constant companion, I've nothing to fear, Hal-le, hal-le - lu - ja!

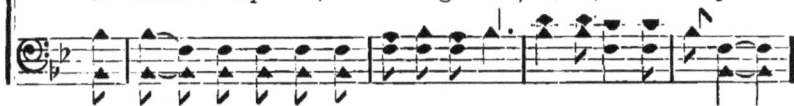

Chorus.

Oh, hal - le - lu - ja! hal - le - lu - ja! I am glad to tell,

Oh, hal - le - lu - ja! hal - le - lu - ja! With my soul 'tis well.

No. 53. ON THE HILLS BEYOND THE RIVER.

Anon.

JAMES A. BUCHANAN.

Andante con espressione.

1. There are hills be-yond the val - ley where the riv - er glid - eth by,
2. On those hills be-yond the riv - er is our heav'nly Father's throne,
3. While we walk a-long the val - ley we may sometimes gain a view

Where the E - den flow'rs are blooming un - der-neath a cloud- less sky;
And the brightness of that cit - y mor- tal eye hath nev- er known;
Of the hills be-yond the riv - er un - der-neath the arch- ing blue;

There the state - ly palms are swaying in the soft and balm- y breeze
Oh its gates are shin - ing brightly in the nev - er fad - ing day
If our foot-steps nev - er fal - ter, in the path that should be trod,

Birds of Par - a-dise are sing- ing from the ev - er ver-dant trees.
For the sun-shine is e - ter - nal and can nev - er fade a- way.
We may one day claim a dwell-ing in the cit - y of our God.

On the Hills Beyond the River.—Concluded.

Chorus.

On the hills . . . . beyond the riv - er, state - ly
On the hills beyond the riv - er, on the hills beyond the riv - er, stately

hills, ... ma-jes - tic hills; We shall
hills beyond the riv - er, state - ly hills, ma - jes - tic hills; We shall

rest . . . . in peace for - ev - er, on those
rest in peace for ev - er. We shall rest in peace on those

hills, ... en-dur-ing hills; We shall rest . . . . . in peace for -
hills, enduring hills, endur - ing hills; We shall rest in peace forever, we shall

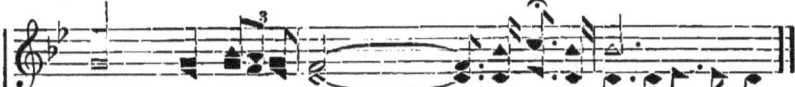

ev - er, on the hills, ... en-dur-ing hills.
rest in peace on the hills, enduring hills, enduring hills, enduring hills.

hills.

Mrs. E. W. CHAPMAN.
J. H. TENNEY.

1. Once for all the Sav-iour His blood hath spilt,
2. Once for all the Fa-ther, His Son hath giv'n.
3. Once for all, O sin-ner, this grace re-ceive,

On the cross of Cal-va-ry, On the cross of Cal-va-ry;
Man to res-cue by His grace, Man to res-cue by His grace;
Let the hopes of heav'n be thine, Let the hopes of heav'n be thine:

There the sac-ri-fice that He made for guilt,
Pur-chase for the err-ing, a home in heav'n,
Has-ten now to Je-sus, His word be-lieve,

Makes the sin-ner pure and free. . . . .
There to see His smil-ing face. . . . .
Safe-ly rest in arms di-vine. . . . . .

ONCE FOR ALL.—Concluded.

Chorus.

Hal - le - lu - jah! . . . Hal - le - lu - jah! . . . .
Hal - le - lu - jah! Hal - le - lu - jah!

Spread the tid - ings o'er this earth - ly ball; . . .

Hal - le - lu - jah! . . . Hal - le - lu - jah! . . .
Hal - le - lu - jah! Hal - le - lu - jah!

Christ, the Lord, hath suf - fered once for all! . . . .

No. 55.   Would The Sinner Ever Turn?

E. R. LATTA.   JNO. R. BRYANT.

1. In the way that leads to death, In the downward way, By the
2. For his feet, how ma-ny snares Wait, up-on the road That would
3. Je-sus pleads with him to stay, And an heir be-come, Of a

pow'r of Satan led, More and more a-stray; There, the sinner, thoughtlessly,
nev-er him be-set, In the path of God! But he is the willing slave
mansion and a crown, In a Heav'nly home; But his heart is set on sin,

Press-es on and on: Feel-ing not, how lost he is, And un-done!
To his great-est foe; And he does not wish to shun End-less woe!
And on pleas-ures, vain: Sin-ner wilt thou from thy Lord Still re-main?

Chorus.

Would the sin-ner ev-er turn From his ways of sin, And for

life e-ter-nal seek, And the vic-t'ry win; If the Spir-it did not woo

Copyright, 1895, by Charlie D. Tillman.

Would The Sinner Ever Turn?—Concluded.

Him in ten - der-ness, And so pa-tient-ly en-treat Him to come?

No. 56. JESUS, SAVIOUR, PILOT ME.

Rev. EDWARD HOPPER, D.D. J. E. GOULD.

1. Je - sus, Sav-iour, pi - lot me, O - ver Life's tempestuous sea,
2. As a moth - er stills her child, Thou canst hush the o-cean wild;
3. When at last I near the shore, And the fear - ful breakers roar

Un-known waves around me roll, Hid - ing rock and treach'rous shoal,
Boist'rous waves o-bey Thy will, When Thou say-est "peace, be still;"
'Twixt me and my peaceful rest, Then while lean-ing on Thy breast,

Chart and com-pass come from Thee, Je - sus, Sav - iour, pi - lot me.
Wond'rous sov'reign of the sea, Je - sus, Sav - iour, pi - lot me.
May I hear Thee say to me, "Fear not, I will pi - lot thee."

No. 57. WHY I LOVE JESUS.

Arranged.

E. O. EXCELL.

1. Would you know why I love Je - sus? Why He is so dear to me?
2. Would you know why I love Je - sus? Why He is so dear to me?
3. Would you know why I love Je - sus? Why He is so dear to me?
4. Would you know why I love Je - sus? Why He is so dear to me?
5. Would you know why I love Je - sus? Why He is so dear to me?

'Tis be-cause my bless- ed Sav- iour From my sins hath set me free.
'Tis be-cause the blood of Je - sus Ful - ly saves and cleans-es me.
'Tis be-cause, a - mid tempta - tion, He supports and strengthens me.
'Tis be-cause, in ev - 'ry con - flict, Je - sus gives me vic - to - ry.
'Tis be-cause, my Friend and Saviour He will ev - er, ev - er be.

Chorus.

This is why.................... Yes, why I love Him, This is
This is why I love my Je - sus, Why I love Him, This is

why.................. I love Him so; He has par -
why I love my Je - sus, Why I love Him so; He has pardon'd, He has

don'd my trans-gres-sions, He has wash'd me white as snow.
par-don'd my trans-gres-sions.

rit.

No. 58. I'VE BEEN WASHED IN THE BLOOD.

Answer to "Are You Washed in the Blood?"

W. T. DALE.   D. E. DORTCH.

1. I have been to Je-sus who has cleans'd my soul, I've been wash'd in the
2. I am dai-ly trusting Je-sus at my side, I've been wash'd in the
3. I am working in the vineyard of the Lord, I've been wash'd in the
4. I am list'ning now to hear the Bridegroom's voice, I've been wash'd in the
5. I am watching for the com-ing of my Lord, I've been wash'd in the

blood of the Lamb, By the blood of Je-sus I have been made whole, I've been
blood of the Lamb, I am sweetly resting in the cru-ci-fied. I've been
blood of the Lamb, I am trusting in the promise of his word, I've been
blood of the Lamb, How His coming will each faithful heart rejoice I've been
blood of the Lamb, He will come according to His faithful word, I've been

D.S.—And my robe is spotless, it is white as snow, I've been

FINE. Chorus.

wash'd in the blood of the Lamb.
wash'd in the blood of the Lamb.   I've been wash'd   I've been
wash'd in the blood of the Lamb.
wash'd in the blood of the Lamb.   in the blood,
wash'd in the blood of the Lamb.

wash'd in the blood of the Lamb.

D.S.

wash'd   I've been wash'd in the blood of the Lamb,
in the blood,   of the Lamb.

Copyright, 1885, by D. E. Dortch, Columbia, Tenn.

SOWING THE TARES.

Dedicated to "Brother Will." M. Cell 1069.

Words by a Convict.　　　　　　　　　　　　　M. A. LEE.

1. Sow-ing the ta res, when it might have been wheat,　Sow-ing of mal - ice,
2. Sow-ing the tares, how dark the black sin,　Mingling a curse with
3. Sow-ing the tares, that bring sor-row down,　Robs of its jew - els
4. Sow-ing the tares, un-der cov- er of night, Which might have been wheat all

spite, and de-ceit, We might have sown roses a - mid life's sad cares, While
life's sweetest hymn, And heeding no anguish, no pit - cous pray'rs, While
life's fair-est crown; And turning to sil-ver the once gold- en hairs, Grown
gold-en and bright; O heart, turn to God with repentance and pray'r And

Refrain.

we were so cru - el - ly sow- ing the tares.
we were so cru - el - ly sow- ing the tares.
whit - er and whit-er as we sowed the tares.
plead for for-giveness for sow-ing the tares.

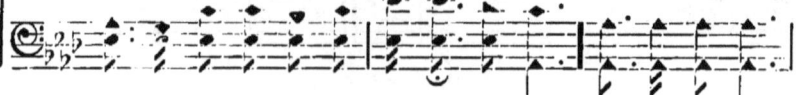

Sow - ing the tares,

Sow- ing the tares, We plead for for-give-ness for sow-ing the tares.

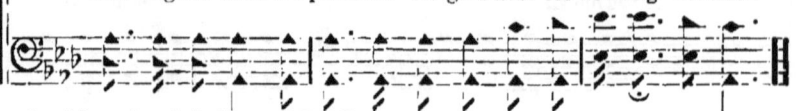

From "Rescue Songs." Used by per. H. H. Hadley.

No. 60.   HIS YOKE IS EASY.

"My yoke is easy and my burden is light."—MATT. 11 : 30.

D. S. WARNER.   B. E. WARREN.

1. I've found my Lord and He is mine, He won me by His love;
2. No oth-er Lord but Christ I know, I walk with Him a-lone;
3. He's dear-er to my heart than life, He found me lost in sin;
4. My flesh re-coiled be-fore the cross, And Sa-tan whispered there,
5. I've tried the road of sin and found Its prospects all de-ceive;

I'll serve Him all my years of time, And dwell with Him a-bove.
His streams of love for-ev-er flow, With-in my heart, His throne.
He calmed the sea of inward strife, And bid me come to Him.
"Thy gain will not re-pay the loss, His yoke is hard to bear."
I've proved the Lord and joys abound, More than I could be-lieve.

Chorus.

His yoke is ea-sy, His burden is light, I've found it so, I've found it so :

His ser-vice is my sweetest delight, His blessings ev-er flow.

No. 61. SCATTERING PRECIOUS SEED.

W. A. OGDEN.　　　　　　　　　　　　　　　GEO. C. HUGG.

1. Scat-ter-ing precious seed by the way-side, Scat-ter-ing precious
2. Scat-ter-ing precious seed for the grow-ing, Scat-ter-ing precious
3. Scat-ter-ing precious seed, doubting nev - er, Scat-ter-ing precious

seed by the hill-side; Scat-ter- ing precious seed o'er the field, wide,
seed, free-ly sow - ing; Scat-ter- ing precious seed, trusting, knowing.
seed, trusting ev - er; Sow-ing the word with pray'r and en-deav-or.

Chorus.

Scat-ter-ing pre-cious seed by the way. ⎱ Sow - ing in the
Sure-ly the Lord will send it the rain. ⎰ Sow - - ing in the
Trusting the Lord for growth and for yield. ⎰ Sowing the precious seed,

morn - - - ing, Sow - - - ing at the
ev - - - 'ning, Sow - - - ing at the
Sow- ing the pre-cious seed, Sow-ing the seed at noon-tide,

noon - - tide; Sow-ing the precious seed by the way . .
Sowing the precious seed; 　　　　　　　　　　　by the way.

pp

No. 62. WONDROUS JOY.

L. E. JONES.   A. J. SHOWALTER.

1. Wondrous joy I have to-day, I'm redeemed, I'm redeemed;
2. Je-sus keeps in per-fect peace, I'm redeemed, I'm redeemed;
3. I can hear my Saviour's voice, I'm redeemed, I'm redeemed;

All my sins are wash'd a-way, I'm re-deemed, I'm redeemed,
Gives from sin a blest re-lease, I'm re-deemed, I'm redeemed,
And it makes my heart re-joice, I'm re-deemed, I'm redeemed,

At the fountain's crim-son flow, I've been cleans'd and now I know,
Long I wandered sore oppressed, But the Sav-iour gave me rest,
Such a friend I nev-er knew, Ev-er pres-ent, ev-er true.

That the blood can wash like snow, I'm re-deemed, I'm redeemed,
Now I'm lean-ing on His breast, I'm re-deemed, I'm redeemed,
He will guide my jour-ney through I'm re-deemed, I'm redeemed,

rit.

That the blood can wash like snow, I'm re-deemed, I'm redeemed.
Now I'm lean-ing on His breast, I'm re-deemed, I'm redeemed.
He will guide my jour-ney through, I'm re-deemed, I'm redeemed.

No. 63. I AM GOING TO A CITY.

(OR THE DYING CHRISTIAN.)

Rev. W. S. McKenzie, D. D.   Rev. F. M. Lamb.

1. I am go-ing to a cit-y, Where my Lord has gone be-fore,
2. I am go-ing to a cit-y, Where my faith will change to sight,
3. I am go-ing to a cit-y, Where the streets are paved with gold,

And a man-sion is pre-par-ing there for me: I will
Out of dark-ness I am pass-ing in to-day; Thro' the
Where the beau-ties are so bril-liant and so rare! Oh, the

serve Him and a-dore Him, I will love Him more and more, When the
val-ley I am tread-ing, But my Sav-iour is my light, And no
gleam-ing walls of jas-per! Oh, the splendors man-i-fold! I am

Chorus.

rich-es of His glo-ry I shall see.)
e-vil shall be-fall me on the way. } I am go-ing to a cit-y,
long-ing, I am sigh-ing to be there.)

Where the liv-ing nev-er die, Where no sick-ness and no

I AM GOING TO A CITY.—Concluded.

rit.

sor-row can mo-lest, From this bod-y to re-lease me He is

speed-ing from on high; He will greet me and es-cort me to my rest.

No. 64. JESUS, THE LIGHT OF THE WORLD.

G. D. E. Arr.

Geo. D. Elderkin. Arr.

1. { Hark! the her - ald an- gels sing, Je- sus, the Light of the world; }
   { Glo - ry to the new born King, [*Omit*. . . . .] }

2. { Joy - ful all ye na-tions rise, Je- sus the Light of the world: }
   { Join the tri-umphs of the skies, [*Omit* . . . .] }

3. { Christ by high - est heav'n adored, Je- sus, the Light of the world, }
   { Christ, the ev - er- last - ing Lord, [*Omit*. . . . .] }

4. { Hail! the heav'n born Prince of peace, Je- sus, the Light of the world; }
   { Hail! the sun of right-eous-ness, [*Omit*. . . . .] }

Fine. Chorus.

Je- sus, the Light of the world. We'll { walk in the light, } Come where the
                                        { beau-ti- ful light. }

Je- sus, the Light of the world.

D. S.

dewdrops of mer- cy are bright, Shine all around us by day and by night,

No. 65. PRAISE HIS NAME.

H. H. S.

HAMP. H. SEWELL.

1. The Sav - iour is the sin - ner's friend, His blood a ran-som
2. O sin - ner hear His lov - ing voice, It speaks to thee and
3. He came to earth a sac - ri - fice That He might sin - ners

for He came . . To die that we might through Him live, And
pleads thy soul . . . Go wash in that soul cleans-ing blood, And
here re - claim . . Oh trust Him now, re - pent, be - lieve, And

I will praise His ho - ly name.
thou shalt then be ful - ly whole.
praise the Saviour's ho - ly name.

I will praise, ... His ho - ly
I will praise His holy name,

name   For His own un - ceas - ing love and His
His ho - ly name

mer - cy from a - bove, I will praise . . . . His ho - ly
I will praise His holy name

PRAISE HIS NAME.—Concluded.

name,   I will praise my Sav-iour's ho - ly name.

His ho - ly name,

No. 66.   RALLY FOR JESUS.

G. W. L.   G. W. Lyon, by per.

With vigor.

1. Ral - ly now for Je - sus, Ral - ly one and all;
2. Has - ten to the con - flict Where His sol - diers stand.
3. Wait not for an - oth - er To de - fend the right,
4. When the war - fare's end - ed And the vic - t'ry won,

Fol - low where He lead - eth, Hear His earn - est call.
Rouse you up to act - ion, It is His com-mand.
Will - ing ser - vice ren - der With your skill and might.
Hear His wel - come greet - ing: "Faith - ful one, well done."

Chorus.

March on . . . to the con - flict, March on . . . in your might.

March on,   in your might,

And drive the foe wher-e'er you go, In the bat - tle for the right.

No. 67. THE DISPENSATION DAY.

B. E. W.

B. E. WARREN.

1. { In the aw - ful age of night, When the earth was struck with blight,
   Per - se - cu - tion's fire and flood, Rag - ing in an an - gry flood,

2. { But she raised her ban - ner high, And did all her foes de - fy,
   For her for - ces mul - ti - plied, Not - with - stand - ing those who died,

3. { Now the eve-'ning time has come, When the bright-ness of the sun,
   It will reach the dis - tant isles, Where the gold - en har-vest smiles,

4. { We are in the eve-'ning light, Shin - ing in the morn-ing light,
   In the con - quest we are strong, Sing - ing as we march a - long,

And the clouds of pap - al dark - ness filled the sky.
(Omit.) . . . . Failed to

O - ver her the gates of hell have not pre - vailed.
(Omit.) . . . . In the

Thro' the gos - pel shines in the re - mot - est land.
(Omit.) . . . . To be

And the clouds of thick ob - scur - i - ty are passed.
(Omit.) . . . . And we're

Chorus.

crush the Church, sustained by God on high.
martyr's flames her glo - ry was revealed.
gathered while the Saviour's near at hand.
read - y for the fi - nal trumpet's blast. }

We are in the evening of the

dis - pen - sa - tion day, And the gos - pel light has scat-tered all the night a-way, On the sun-ny mount-ain hear the

mel-o-dy of song, Float up-on the breez-es, as we swift-ly pass a-long.

No. 68.   HOW I LOVE JESUS.

FREDERICK WHITFIELD.   Arr. by E. O. E.

1. { There is a name I love to hear, I love to sing its worth; It }
   { sounds like music in mine ear, The   (*Omit.*)   } sweetest name on

earth; { Oh, how I love Je-sus,   Oh, how I love Je-sus, }
      { Oh, how I love Je-sus, Be - (*Omit.*)   } cause He first lov'd me.

2 It tells me of a Saviour's love,
　Who died to set me free;
It tells me of His precious blood,
　The sinner's perfect plea.

3 It tells me what my Father hath
　In store for every day,

And, tho' I tread a darksome path,
　Yields sunshine all the way.

4 It tells of One, whose loving heart
　Can feel my deepest woe,
Who in each sorrow bears a part,
　That none can bear below.

7

CHILDREN'S SONG.

M. B. J.   J. R. B.

1. Lit-tle [1]hands to [2]work in the [3]Mas-ter's [4]vineyard, Lit-tle [5]feet to
2. Lit-tle will [11]that ev - er will keep me [12]do - ing, Lit-tle [13]eyes to
3. Lit-tle [20]knees to bow at the bless - ed al - tar, Lit-tle [21]lips to

[6]walk in the bless - ed [7]way; Lit - tle [8]heart with life from the
[14]see lest I [15]faint and [16]fall; Lit - tle [17]mind to [18]learn of the
smile when His face I [22]see; Lit - tle [23]ears to [24]hear when He

[9]lov - ing Sav-iour, Lit - tle [10]tongue to speak of His love each day.
Saviour's [19]precepts, Lit-tle voice to sing forth His prais - es all.
speaks so ten - der, Lit - tle [25]soul to save for e - ter - ni - ty.

Chorus.

Oh, the lit - tle deeds can be done for Je - sus. Oh, the lit - tle

songs we can al - ways sing; Oh, the pre-cious love that He

CHILDREN'S SONG.—Concluded.

pours up - on · us, When our lit - tle trib - ute to Him we bring.

Gestures to "CHILDREN'S SONG."

1. Extending hands.
2. Striking with both hands.
3. Left hand raised, right, extended,
4. Right pointing to the right.
5 & 6. Two steps forward placing even again.
7. Motioning right hand forward.
8. Right hand to heart.
9. Both hands raised beckoning.
10. Left forefinger to lips.
11. Showing both palms.
12. Motioning both hands to the left.
13. Covering eyes with left hand.
14. Peering forward.
15. Swaying body forward.
16. Casting both hands to left, downward
17. Left hand clasping forehead.
18. Both hands raised, thrown out in opposite directions.
19. Both hands thrown out.
20. Kneeling down.
21. Left hand to lips.
22. Peering upward.
23. Left hand to ear turning face a little to the right.
24. Folding arms.

No. 70. LITTLE SOLDIERS.

HAZEL MITCHELL, age 10 years.

H. M. Har. by JOHN McPHERSON. By per.

Moderato.

1. Brave lit- tle sol-diers we must be, If the face of our Lord we see;
2. As I now walk within His path, He will keep me from sin and wrath;
3. Sure I am Je- sus' friend to-day, For He leads me a-long the way;
4. Marching along to heav'n's sweet land, Walking on at our Lord's command,

CHO.—O, I love Je- sus, yes, I do, And I know that He loves me too;

D. C. for Chorus.

If we are faith- ful to the end, We shall live with Him.
No mat- ter if the way seem dim, I will fol - low Him.
And tho' temp- ta- tious sore may come, I will keep with Him.
We'll bear the cross and wear the crown, When we live with Him.

To me what-ev - er He may say, Glad - ly I'll o - bey.

No. 71. KEEP CLOSE TO JESUS.

J. L.

John Lane, by per. 1892.

1. When you start for the land of heav-en-ly rest, Keep close to
2. Nev-er mind the storms or tri-als as you go, Keep close to
3. To be safe from the darts of the e - vil one, Keep close to
4. We shall reach our home in heav-en by and by, Keep close to

Je-sus all the way; For He is the Guide, and He knows the way best,
Je-sus all the way; 'Tis a comfort and joy, His fa-vor to know,
Je-sus all the way; Take the shield of faith till the vict'ry is won,
Je-sus all the way; Where to those we love we'll never say good-bye,

Chorus.

Keep close to Je-sus all the way. Keep close to Je-sus,

Keep close to Je-sus, Keep close to Je-sus all the way; By

day or by night never turn from the right, Keep close to Jesus all the way.

No. 72. WHEN I SEE THE BLOOD.

JOHN.   J. G. F.

1. Christ our Re-deem-er died on the cross, Died for the sin-ner,
2. Chief-est of sin-ners, Je-sus can save, As He has prom-ised,
3. Judg-ment is com-ing, all will be there, Who have re-ject-ed,
4. O. what com-pas-sion, oh bound-less love! Je-sus hath pow-er,

paid all His due; All who re-ceive Him need nev-er fear,
so will He do; Oh, sin-ner, hear Him, trust in His word,
who have refused? Oh, sin-ner, has-ten, let Je-sus in.
Je-sus is true; All who be-lieve are safe from the storm,

Chorus.

Yes, He will pass, will pass o-ver you. When I   see the
Then He will pass, will pass o-ver you.
Then God will pass, will pass o-ver you.
Oh, He will pass, will pass o-ver you.   When I

blood,.   When I   see the blood,   When I   see the
see the blood.   When I   see the blood,   When I

rit.

blood,   I will pass, I will pass o-ver you.
see the blood.   o-ver you.

No. 73. SPEAK JUST A WORD.

L. R. M.

LUCY RIDER MEYER.

1. Speak just a word for your Mas-ter and your Lord, Speak just a word,
2. Speak just a word when a-bout your dai-ly task, Speak just a word,
3. Speak just a word, for wher-ev-er you may go, Speak just a word,
4. Speak just a word, if a "cross" it seems to be, Speak just a word,

REF.—Speak just a word, He will teach you what to say, Speak just a word,

speak just a word; Stand in His name, let your loy-al voice be heard;
speak just a word; He giv-eth grace un - to all who tru-ly ask,
speak just a word; Sad hearts are long-ing the way of life to know,
speak just a word; Think of the *true* cross upraised on Cal - va - ry,

speak just a word; His the re-sult, ours is on-ly to o-bey.

FINE.

Speak just a word for Je - sus. Speak just a word, oh, con -
Speak just a word for Je - sus. He calls you friend, oh, the
Speak just a word for Je - sus. Some lit - tle word He may
Speak just a word for Je - sus. Lift up the ban - ner of

Speak just a word for Je - sus.

pp   *ff*

fess your Saviour King; He list-ens, listens near; Oh, nev-er, nev - er fear;
wonders of His grace! He list-ens, listens near: Oh, nev-er, nev-er, fear;
use to cheer and bless, He list-ens, listens near; Oh, nev-er, nev - er fear;
Him who died for you, He list-ens, listens near; Oh, nev-er, nev - er fear;

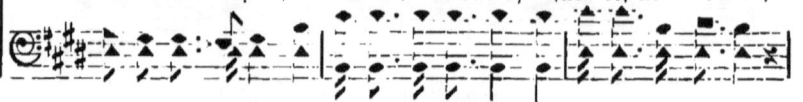

SPEAK JUST A WORD.—Concluded.

D.C.

Come, to His al-tar a sac-ri-fice to bring, Speak just a word for Je-sus.
Talk of your Lord and His love in ev'ry place, Speak just a word for Je-sus.
Some little word He may use to cheer and bless, Speak just a word for Je-sus.
He calls for witnesses, loyal hearts and true, Speak just a word for Je-sus.

No. 74.   THE GOSPEL FEAST.

"Come, for all things are ready."—LUKE 14 : 16.

CHARLES WESLEY.
Cho. by H. L. G.

H. L. GILMOUR.

1. Come, sinners, to the gos-pel feast; It is for you, it is for me;
2. Ye need not one be left be-hind, It is for you, it is for me;

FINE.

Let ev-'ry soul be Jesus' guest; It is for you, it is for me.
For God hath bid-den all mankind, It is for you, it is for me.

D.S.—O wea-ry wand'rer, come and see, It is for you, it is for me.

Chorus.

D.S.

Sal - va-tion full, sal - va-tion free, The price was paid on Cal - va-ry;

3 Sent by my Lord, on you I call:
  The invitation is to all:
4 Come, all the world! come, sinner, thou!
  All things in Christ are ready now.
5 Come, all ye souls by sin oppressed,
  Ye restless wanderers after rest;
6 Ye poor, and maimed, and halt, and blind
  In Christ a hearty welcome find.

7 My message as from God receive;
  Ye all may come to Christ and live:
8 O let this love your hearts constrain,
  Nor suffer Him to die in vain.
9 See Him set forth before your eyes,
  That precious, bleeding sacrifice:
10 His offered benefits embrace,
  And freely now be saved by grace.

No. 75. MY MOTHER'S BIBLE.

M. B. WILLIAMS. CHARLIE D. TILLMAN.

DUET.

1. There's a dear and pre-cious book, Tho' its worn and fa-ded now,
2. As she read the sto-ries o'er, Of those might-y men of old,
3. Then she read of Je - sus, love, As he blest the chil-dren dear,
4. Well, those days are past and gone, But their mem'ry lin-gers still,

Which re - calls those hap - py days of long a - go;
Of Jos - eph and of Dan - iel and their trials;
How he suf-fered, bled and died up - on the tree;
And the dear old Book each day has been my guide;

When I stood at moth-er's knee, With her hand up-on my brow,
Of lit - tle Da - vid bold, Who be - came a king at last;
Of his heav-y load of care, Then she dried my flow-ing tears
And I seek to do his will, As my mo-ther taught me then,

And I heard her voice in gen - tle tones and low.
Of Sa - tan with his ma - ny wick - ed wiles.
With her kiss - es as she said it was for me.
And ev - er in my heart His words a - bide.

MY MOTHER'S BIBLE.—Concluded.

CHORUS.

Bless-ed book,...... . precious book,........ On thy dear old tear-stained
Blessed book, precious book,

leaves I love to look; (love to look;) Thou art sweet-er day by day,

As I walk the narrow way That leads at last to that bright home above.

No. 76. *Key of F.*

1 What a Friend we have in Jesus,
  All our sins and griefs to bear!
What a privilege to carry
  Every thing to God in prayer!
Oh, what peace we often forfeit,
  Oh, what needless pain we bear--
All because we do not carry
  Every thing to God in prayer.

2 Have we trials and temptations?
  Is there trouble anywhere?
We should never be discouraged,
  Take it to the Lord in prayer.
Can we find a friend so faithful,
  Who will all our sorrows share?
Jesus knows our every weakness;
  Take it to the Lord in prayer.

No. 77. *Key of F.*

1 Work, for the night is coming,
  Work through the morning hours;
Work while the dew is sparkling,
  Work 'mid springing flowers;
Work when the day grows brighter,
  Work in the glowing sun;
Work, for the night is coming,
  When man's work is done.

2 Work, for the night is coming,
  Work through the sunny noon;
Fill brightest hours with labor,
  Rest comes sure and soon;
Give every flying minute
  Something to keep in store;
Work, for the night is coming,
  When man works no more.

No. 78.   THE LIFE-BOAT.

First 3 verses ANON.
Last 4 by Rev. M. M. BRABHAM.

Arr. by JNO. R. BRYANT.

SOLO.

1. We're float-ing down the stream of time, We have not long to stay;
2. Sometimes we've felt dis-cour-ag-ed, And thought it all in vain,
3. The Life-boat soon is com-ing, By the eye of Faith I see,

The storm-y clouds of dark-ness Will turn to brightest day.
For us to live a Christian life, And walk in Je-sus' name.
As she sweeps thro' the wa-ters To res-cue you and me,

Then let us all take cour-age, For we're not left a - lone;
But then we heard the Mas-ter say, I'll lend a help-ing hand;
And land us safe-ly in the port With friends we love so dear.

The life-boat soon is com - ing To gath-er the jew-els home.
And if you'll on-ly trust me I'll guide you to that land.
"Get read-y," cries the Cap - tain. Oh! look, she is al-most here.

THE LIFE-BOAT.—Concluded.

CHORUS.

Then cheer, my brother, cheer. Our tri-als will soon be o'er. Our lov'd ones we will
We're pilgrims and we're strangers here, We're seeking a city to come. The life-boat soon is

1 meet. will meet Up-on the gold-en shore;
2 com - ing To gath-er the jew-els home.

4 Yes, see her coming o'er the tide
  With banners all unfurled;
  She comes from heavenly ports
    afar,
  To take us from this world.
  "Aboard, aboard," the Captain cries,
  Let every pilgrim come,
  And once upon the Life-boat,
  I'll bear you safely home."

5 Behold all things are ready now,
  The bells begin to ring,
  The Captain stands upon the prow,
  And all the pilgrims sing.
  The breezes fill the canvas,
  The waters rush and foam,
  For we're upon the Life-boat,
  And on our journey home.

6 Far out upon the widening seas
  Our Captain steers the way,
  And yonder in the eastern skies
  We see the gleaming day.
  Oh, yes, we see the distant shore,
  We hear the ransomed sing,
  And every breeze that comes this way
  The sweetest odors bring.

7 Oh, wondrous joy we're home at last,
  We've reached the golden shore!
  And here we'll live, and sing, and
    praise,
  And shout forever more.
  We're welcomed by our Saviour here
  And friends and loved ones come;
  While angel throngs and ransomed
  All bid us welcome home!   [saints

No. 79. Sinners, Turn; Why Will Ye Die?

REV. C. WESLEY, 1745.

1 Sinners, turn; why will ye die?
God, your Maker, asks you why?
God, who did your being give,
Made you with Himself to live;
He the fatal cause demands:
Asks the work of His own hands,—
Why, ye thankless creatures, why
Will ye cross His love, and die?

3 Sinners, turn; why will ye die?
God, your Saviour, asks you why?
He, who did your souls retrieve,
Died Himself, that ye might live.

Will ye let Him die in vain?
Crucify your Lord again?
Why, ye ransomed sinners, why
Will ye slight His grace and die?

3 Sinners, turn; why will ye die?
God, the Spirit, asks you why?
He who all your lives hath strove,
Urged you to embrace His love.
Will ye not His grace receive?
Will ye still refuse to live?
O ye dying sinners, why,
Why will ye forever die?

No. 80. SOMETHING JESUS GAVE ME.

GRACE W. HINSDALE.   W. A. OGDEN. By per.

Effective as a Solo.

1. I have some-thing Je - sus gave me for my own (my own);
2. Like His pres - ence it doth bring me peace di - vine (di - vine);
3. If my hu - man hands had found it, I should grieve (should grieve);

It is some-thing which He sent me from His throne (from His throne);
'T is His sweet and ten - der whis - per, thou art Mine (thou art mine);
But my Sav - iour gave it to me, I be - lieve (I be - lieve);

It is some-thing which I car - ry in my heart (my heart);
What's the gift I clasp so fond - ly,would'st thou see (thou see)?
Oh, how sweet it is to bear it as His gift (His gift),

It is safe till Je - sus bids me from it part (it part).
'T is a cross which Christ,my Mas - ter, gave to me (to me).
While the bur - den of my sor - row Christ doth lift (doth lift).

REFRAIN.

'T is a cross .. He gave me. All in love .. He gave me,
A cross yes. In love

SOMETHING JESUS GAVE ME.—Concluded.

To have, . . to bear, . . In meekness and in prayer.
To have, to bear,

No. 81. JESUS IS PASSING.

L. L. PICKETT.   Words of Chorus from SALVATION ARMY.   L. L. PICKETT.

1. Come, sin - ner, hast - en to the cross, The Sav-iour bids you come ; Come,
2. De - lay no long-er, come to - day, Ac-cept Him and be - lieve ; And
3. The purchase price He ful - ly paid On Cal-v'ry's cru - el tree ; With

trust - ing in His pre - cious blood ; Wait not—there still is room.
He will par - don ev - 'ry sin, And all your fears re - lieve.
His own blood He ran-somed you From end - less mis - er - y.

CHORUS. *faster.*

Je - sus now is pass - ing by, pass - ing by, pass - ing by,
While He is so ver - y nigh, ver - y nigh, ver - y nigh,

Je - sus now is pass - ing by, I 'll go out and meet Him.
While He is so ver - y nigh, I 'll go out and greet Him.

4 Oh, turn to Him with all your heart,
    And yield at once your will ;
  He long has sought to save your soul,
    He waits in mercy still.

5 But if you still His calls refuse,
    Fearful will be the cost ;
  Your days of grace will soon be o'er,
    And you forever lost.

No. 82. MY FEET ARE ON THE HIGHWAY.

L. E. J.

L. E. Jones.
Arr. Charlie D. Tillman.

1. My feet are on the highway I am marching on to-day, Hal - le -
2. My feet are on the highway where the rays of glo - ry shine,
3. My feet are on the highway and the Saviour's love I know, Hal - le -

lu - - iah! Hal - le - lu - - iah! I have found the Saviour
All the way my steps are
lu-iah! Praise His name, Hallelujah! Praise His name, I am walking where He

precious since He wash'd my sins away, Hal- le - lu - iah! praise His name.
guid-ed by a pow'r that is di-vine, Hal- le - lu - iah! praise His name.
leads me, and re-joic-ing as I go, Hal- le - lu - iah! praise His name.

Chorus.

Hal- le - lu - - iah! Hal- le - lu - - iah! My feet are on the
Hal - le - lu-iah!   Hal- le -lu-iah!

highway of the King,   I am hap- py in His ser-vice and I
of the King,

MY FEET ARE ON THE HIGHWAY.—Concluded.

can-not help but sing, Hal-le - lu - iah! praise His name! (His holy name!

No. 83. I COULD NOT DO WITHOUT THEE.

FRANCES R. HAVERGAL. SIGISMUND THALBERG.

Andante.

1. I could not do with-out Thee, O Sav-iour of the lost,
2. I could not do with-out Thee, I can-not stand a - lone;
3. I could not do with-out Thee, For years are fleet -ing fast,

Whose pre- cious blood redeemed me At such tre- men-dous cost;
I have no strength or good - ness, No wis - dom of my own;
And soon in sol - emn si - lence The riv - er must be passed;

Thy right-eousness, thy par - don, thy sac - ri - fice, must be . .
But Thou, be - lov - ed Sav - iour, Art all in all to me, . .
But Thou wilt nev - er leave me, And, tho' the waves run high, .

rit.

My on - ly hope and com - fort, My glo - ry and my plea.
And weakness will be pow - er, If lean - ing hard on Thee.
I know Thou wilt be near me, And whis -per "It is I."

No. 84.   THE *NEW CAMP GROUND.

D. S. WARNER.   B. E. WARREN.

1. We have met to-day on the new camp ground, And our hearts, O God o'erflow.
2. We have met to-day on the new camp ground, And our shouts of glory ring;
3. We have met to-day on the new camp ground, Oh, the fellowship so sweet!
4. We have met to-day on the new camp ground, And we come in Jesus' name:
5. We have met to-day on the new camp ground, And we come to work and pray,

With our songs of joy, and a stream of thanks, For the love Thou dost bestow.
There's a might-y stir as the Lord comes down, And the saints of God pour in.
As the pure in heart all to-geth- er flow, In the bonds of love complete.
Here, oh, mighty God, let Thy thunder sound, And Thy aw-ful Spir-it flame.
Here, redeem, dear Lord, even in multitudes, At Thy al - tars day by day.

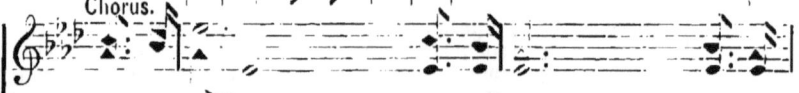

Chorus.

We will sing,   praise the Lord;   Let the
           hal - le - lu - jah!   praise the Lord,

joy - ful   mu - sic   roll;   We will strike   the hap - py   key.

hal - le - lu - jah I   am   free! We will sing   in   sweet ac- cord.

* Old can be used instead of new.

ONE NARROW WAY.

B. E. F.

JOHN 14 : 6; 10 : 9.

BIRDIE E. FINK.

Slow with expressione.

1. On - ly *one* narrow, way. "I am *the* way," On - ly *one*
2. On - ly *one* mind and mouth, All speak the same, On - ly *one*
3. Oh, see His crim-son blood, Flow - ing for all; Be - hold thy

o- pen door, "I am *the* door," On - ly *one* Shepherd, kind,
church of God, Kept in His name. On - ly *one* gen- tle hand,
patient friend, Drink-ing life's gall. On - ly *one* rest complete,

To heal the sick and blind, On - ly *one* reek - ing cross,
To lead the lit - tle band; On - ly *one* ho - ly plain,
Low at His love - ly feet; On - ly *one* fount-ain free,

Refrain.

For souls that are lost. ⎫
One heav - en to gain. ⎬ On - ly *one* nar - row way,
'Tis flow - ing for thee. ⎭

"I am *the* way," On - ly *one* o- pen' door, "I am *the* door."

No. 86. THERE'S A FOUNTAIN OF BLOOD.

"In that day there shall be a fountain opened . . for sin and uncleanness."—ZECH. 13: 1.

D. S. WARNER.　　　　　　　　　　　　　　　　B. E. WARREN.

1. { There's a fount - ain of blood That a - tones for the soul, And it
   { Oh, the dear Lamb of God Makes me per - fect - ly whole, (*Omit.*)

2. { Oh, the vir - tue di-vine, Oh, the soul-cleansing tide! Here the
   { And to - day is the time, Lo! the spir - it and bride (*Omit.*)

3. { Oh, my heart o - ver-flows As I sing of the blood, That has
   { And the light ev - er glows In the tem - ple of God; (*Omit.*)

flows from the side of the Lord;　For I stand on the rock of His word.
vil - est may wash and be clean;　Bid you come to the all-cleansing stream.
washed me so heav- en - ly pure;　All redeemed in the blood ev - er-more.

Chorus.

In the blood,　　　　　　　　in the blood,　　　　　Praise the
In the blood, of the Lamb, oh, the blood of the Lamb!

Lord! I'm redeemed unto God, (thro' the blood,) Oh, this moment I know I am

whit - er than snow, I am wash'd in the blood of the Lamb, (of the Lamb.)

No. 87. WE SHALL RUN AND NOT BE WEARY.

Is. 40 : 31.

B. E. W.   B. E. WARREN.

1. I now am running in the Christian race, To gain the promised prize;
2. We'll run and nev-er fal-ter by the way, For Je-sus' word is true;
3. I'll stand up-on His word and prove His pow'r, The Rock of A-ges past;
4. The heav-y weights of sin are laid a-side, My heart is free and light;
5. When life is o'er and la-bor here is done, Can we thus say with Paul?—

Through Je-sus' matchless, saving, keeping grace, We'll crown Him in the skies.
He's promised if we ev-er will o-bey, To bring us safe-ly through.
I know He'll keep me, trusting ev-'ry hour, While life on earth shall last.
There's nothing we may fear which can be-tide Our hope is clear and bright.
"I've fought the fight and there's a starry crown," That's waiting for us all.

Chorus.

We shall run . . . . . . and not be wea - ry,
We shall run and not be wea - ry we shall walk and nev-er faint;

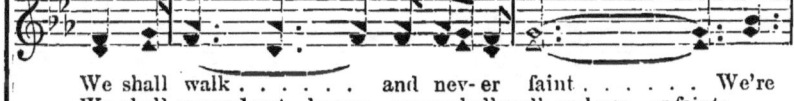

We shall walk . . . . . and nev-er faint . . . . . . We're
We shall run and not be wea-ry, we shall walk and nev - er faint;

trav'ling to our hap-py home, We'll walk and nev-er faint, (never faint.)

No. 88. JESUS IS PLEADING FOR THEE.

B. E. W.

B. E. WARREN.

1. Hear the gen-tle spir-it's call, Je-sus is pleading for thee;
2. Sin-ner, will you come to-day? Je-sus is pleading for thee;
3. Oh! He drank that bit-ter cup, Je-sus is pleading for thee:
4. He will wash your garments white, Je-sus is pleading for thee:
5. He will sweep your guilt a-way, Je-sus is pleading for thee:
6. He will give you joy and peace, Je-sus is pleading for thee;

There is par-don free for all, Je-sus is plead-ing for thee.
Leave that dark and drear-y way, Je-sus is plead-ing for thee.
And this world you must give up, Je-sus is plead-ing for thee.
Turn your darkness in-to light, Je-sus is plead-ing for thee.
Make thy soul as clear as day, Je-sus is plead-ing for thee.
Glo-ry that will nev-er cease, Je-sus is plead-ing for thee.

Chorus.

Wash   in   the blood,.. Wash in the blood of Je-sus;
Wash in the blood of the cleansing tide,

Wash   in   the blood, Wash in the blood of the Lamb...
Wash in the blood of the cleansing tide,   of the Lamb.

No. 89. STEP IN THE LIFE-BOAT.

PERLA E. HIGGINS.   D. E. DORTCH.

1. The life-boat is launch'd on the wild, storm-y sea, To res-cue the
2. The life-boat is launch'd, it is now at your side; Christ's hands are out-
3. The life-boat is launch'd, she is tak - ing us home, While thousands are

lost who are drift-ing a - way; For Sa - tan is striv-ing their
stretch'd to af - ford you re - lief; Ac - cept the kind aid and be
drift-ing to end - less de-spair; O, broth-er. come with us, sal-

Rit.

souls to obtain, While Je - sus is call-ing, "I'll save you to-day."
rescued from death; Re-ject-ing is choosing your soul's endless grief.
va-tion is free; The Sav-iour will par-don, sub - mit to His care.

Chorus.

Step in the life-boat, step in the life-boat, Jesus invites you no long-er de-lay;

Rit.

Step in the life-boat, step in the life-boat, Jesus is calling, "I'll save you to-day."

No. 90. COME TO THE SAVIOUR.

"And him that cometh to me I will in no wise cast out."—John 6: 37

Rev. Elisha A. Hoffman.　　　　　　　　　　　A. F. Myers.

Moderato.

1. Je - sus is call- ing, call- ing for thee, Hear- est thou not His im -
2. Je - sus is pleading, pleading with thee, Was ev - er mer- cy so
3. Je - sus is wait- ing, wait- ing for thee, Love could not pur- er and
4. Je - sus is here but soon He may go, Shall He bear with Him thy

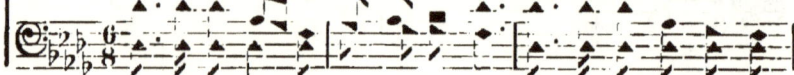

por- tu- nate plea? Oh, by the spear-wound pierced in His side. Haste to be
rich and so free? Wonder-ful grace He waits to be- stow, Is it not
ho - li - er be. Oh, for the blood poured out for thy soul, Come to this
sins and thy woe? Oh, then en-treat Him, ere He de- part. Free- ly to

Chorus.

saved by the cru - ci- fied. 1st. Come to the Saviour, no lon- ger de - lay,
strange He should love thee so?

Sav-iour and be made whole.　　*Last Chorus.*

par-don and cleanse thy heart. Wonderful grace! how it sat - is- fies me,

Trust in His love and ac- cept Him to - day; Ten-der-ly, lov- ing- ly
Won-der-ful mer-cy! so rich and so free; Would you a child of the

calls He to thee, List to His pleading, be - lieve and be free.
cov - e - nant be? Je- sus can save you—he sweet- ly saved me.

No. 91. I KNOW MY NAME IS THERE.

"Rejoice because your names are written in heaven."—LUKE 10 : 20.

D. S. WARNER.   B. E. WARREN. By per.

1. My name is in the Book of life, Oh, bless the name of Je - sus!
2. My name once stood with sinners, lost, And bore a pain-ful rec - ord;
3. Yet in-ward trouble oft - en cast A shad-ow o'er my ti - tle;
4. While others climb thro' worldly strife, To carve a name of hon - or,

I rise a - bove all doubt and strife, And read my ti - tle clear.
But, by His blood the Sav-iour crossed, And placed it on His roll.
But, now with full sal - va-tion blest, Praise God! its ev - er clear.
High up in Heaven's Book of life, My name is writ-ten there.

Chorus.

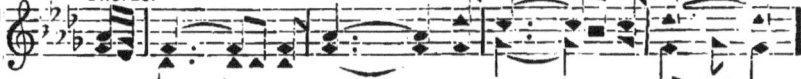

I know, . . I know . . my name . . is there; . .
I know, I tru - ly know, I know my name is there,

I know, I know . . . my name is writ-ten there.
I know my name is there,

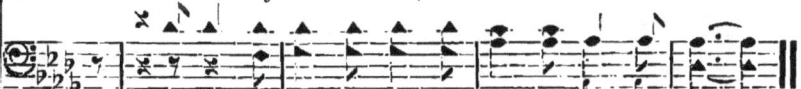

Second No. 90. *Music on opposite page.*

Glory to Jesus.

1 If you want pardon, if you want peace,
  If you want sorrow and sighing to cease,
  Look to the Saviour who died on the tree,
  Jesus can save you, for He saved me.

CHORUS.

Glory to Jesus, He satisfies me.
  Glory to Jesus, I'm free, I am free,
Glory to Jesus, I'll shout it, I will,
  Glory to Jesus, I cannot keep still.

2 Living beneath the shade of the cross,
  Counting the jewels of earth all as dross,
  Cleansed in the blood flowing free from His side,
  Jesus can save you, for you He died.

3 If you want boldness, take part in the fight;
  If you want purity, walk in the light,
  If you want liberty, shout and be free,
  Jesus can cleanse you, for He cleans'd me.

4 If you want Jesus to reign in your soul,
  Plunge in the fountain and you shall be whole,
  Washed in the blood of the crucified, He,
  Jesus can cleanse you, for He cleans'd me.

No. 92. THE MASTER CALLS FOR REAPERS.

M. W. KNAPP.　　　　　　　　　　　　　　　　　　L. L. PICKETT.

1. { Hark! the Mas - - - ter calls for reap - - - ers; Rich and
   { I - dle not, ... but quick-ly fly - - - ing, An-swer,

1. { Hark! the Mas-ter calls for reap-ers, calls for reap-ers;
   { I - dle not, but quick-ly fly - ing, quick-ly fly - ing,

ripe . . . the harvest, see. . . . . . . }
Lord, . . send me, send me. . . . . . }　　CHORUS.

Rich and ripe the harvest, see, the harvest, see; }
Answer, Lord, send me, send me, O Lord, send me. }　Spread the gospel in - vi-

Spread the gos - - pel in - vi-

ta - tion,　　　Speak a warn - ing, breathe a prayer;

ta - tion. Speak a warn - - ing, breathe a prayer, All a-

All around you men are dy - ing,　　You can find them ev'ry where.

round . . . you men are dy - ing, You can find . . . them ev'ry-where.

2 Great the harvest, few the toilers,
Work is waiting one and all;
Answer quickly, and rejoicing,
Hear and heed the Master's call.

3 Gather golden sheaves for Jesus,
Ere too late, they ruined be;
Great and precious is the harvest,
And 't is Jesus calleth thee.

4 Rich reward is for thee waiting,
If but faithful thou wilt prove;

Christ will say, "Well done, thou faith-
In His kingdom bright above. [ful,"

5 But if thou shouldst falsely linger,
Proving thus to Him untrue,
Fearful, then, will be the reckoning
At the Judgment waiting you.

6 Jesus shed His blood so precious,
On the cross for thee didst die;
Therefore heed His call so earnest,
Swiftly to the harvest fly.

No. 93. THROW OUT THE LIFE-LINE.

Rev. E. S. Ufford.   Rev. E. S. Ufford.

1. Throw out the Life-Line a-cross the dark wave, There is a brother whom
2. Throw out the Life-Line with hand quick and strong, Why do you tar-ry, my
3. Throw out the Life-Line to danger-fraught men, Sink-ing in anguish where
4. Soon will this sea-son of res-cue be o'er, Soon we shall go to the

some one should save; Some-bod-y's broth-er, O who then will dare
broth-er, so long? See, he is sink-ing, O has-ten to-day,
we've nev-er been; Winds of temp-ta-tion and bil-lows of woe,
fair E-den shore; Then in the dark hour of death may it be,

Chorus.

To throw out the Life-Line, his per-il to share? Throw out the Life-Line!
And out with the life-boat, a-way, then, a-way.
Will soon hurl them out where the dark wa-ters flow.
That Je-sus will throw out the Life-Line to thee.

throw out the Life-Line! Some one is drift-ing a-way; Throw out the

Life-Line! throw out the Life-Line! Some one is sink-ing to-day.

Copyright, 1888, by Rev. E. S. Ufford. By permission.

No. 94. THE MUSIC OF HIS NAME.

"Sing for the honor of His Name."— Ps. 66 : 2.

D. S. WARNER.   B. E. WARREN.

1. Who can sing the wondrous love of the Son Di - vine? Oh! my
2. Tune your hearts, ye ransomed throng, and ex - tol the Christ: Sing the
3. Oh! let saints and an - gels join in tri-umph-ant song; Let the

Lord, there's none so dear to me, As the One who bore the
name that o - pened mer - cy's door. Oh! 'tis mu - sic, sweet - est
mu - sic of all worlds ac - cord, And in ho - ly an - thems

bur - den of all my sin, And so free - ly died to set me free.
mu - sic to sin - ners lost, Sweet-est to the saints for - ev - er - more.
high o - ver all, pro-claim. Glo - ry be to Je - sus Christ the Lord.

Chorus.

Oh, the pre-cious   mu - sic of Je - sus'   name!
Oh, the pre-cious, pre-cious mu - sic of Je - sus' ho - ly name!

Glo - ry   to   the   Lamb!   Oh, sweetest name in song!
Glo - ry glo-ry to the precious Lamb, precious Lamb.

THE MUSIC OF HIS NAME.—Concluded.

All the heav-ens shall prolong The mu - sic of Thy name. (of Thy name.

No. 95.   ENOUGH FOR ME.

Words and Music by Rev. E. A. HOFFMAN, by per.

1. O love sur-pass - ing knowledge! O grace so full and free!
2. O won - der- ful sal - va - tion! From sin He makes me free!
3. O blood of Christ so pre-cious, Poured out on Cal - va - ry!

FINE.

I know that Je - sus saves me, And that's e-nough for me!
I feel the sweet as - sur-ance, And that's e-nough for me!
I feel its cleans-ing pow - er, And that's e-nough for me!

D.S.—I know that Je - sus saves me, And that's e-nough for me!

Refrain.   D.S.

And that's e - nough for me! And that's e - nough for me!

4 Oh, wondrous love of Jesus,
   He tasted death for me;
   He lives my King forever,
   And that's enough for me.

5 His blessed Holy Spirit
   With mine doth now agree;
   He tells me—I'm adopted;
   And that's enough for me.

6 I have His sweet communion,
   He walks—and talks with me,
   And fills my life with gladness—
   And that's enough for me.

7 His grace will be sufficient,
   Till I His glory see.
   Then safe at home forever—
   And that's enough for me.

No. 96.   CONVERTS PRAISES.

E. S. U.

EDWARD S. UFFORD.

1. I can join the Con-verts prais-es, For I've been re-deem'd from sin;
2. I can feel the heavenly wit- ness, Speaking si - lent bless-ing now;
3. I can look toward the fu - ture, When my feet are mov- ing fast.

I can sing a wond'rous sto - ry, Calm without and peace within.
I can know that Je- sus lis- tens, When be-fore His throne I bow.
I can al- most hear the voic- es, As they whis-per, "Home at last."

FINE.

D.S.—I am now re-deem'd from sin— Calm without and peace within.

Chorus.

I can sing, I can pray, All my doubts and fears a - way;

Used by per. of Author.

No. 97.   PRAYS FOR HER BOY.

TUNE—"Old Oaken Bucket."

1 Oh, who can forget the kind care of a mother?
   A Mother who kneels down and prays for her boy,
Who weeps at the altar and pleads as no other,
   For one gone astray who has blighted her joy.
How anxious she watches when late home returning,
   To see if the tempter was leading astray;
She's fearing and dreading her loving heart yearning,
   Oh, what more can she do, but kneel there and pray.

REFRAIN.—O she prays for her darling, with heart almost breaking;
   A mother who prays for her own precious boy.

2 How pale was her face, when her boy would come reeling,
   With his wild foolish talking, that chilled her dear heart,
How little he thinks of her poor wounded feelings,
   Struggling to keep back the tears that do start.
She even could wish the death-angel had taken,
   When safely to heaven he could have been borne;
She sees her kind teachings, he has now forsaken,
   He thoughtlessly leaves her to pray and to mourn.

LAST REFRAIN.—Come now to mother's Saviour and He will receive you;
   If you come repentant he'll cleanse you from sin.

CHARLIE D. TILLMAN from G. W. PAYNE.

No. 98.   DARE TO BE A PAUL.

To T. De Witt Talmage, D. D. whose few words of personal encouragement have not been lost nor forgotten. This hymn is respectfully dedicated by the author.

Words and music by Rev. E. S. UFFORD.

1. See that lonely pris-on- er, There in   Fe - lix's hall,   Hear him tell the
2. See that no-ble pris-on- er, Stand-ing there a - lone,   Pleading in his
3. See that hap-py pris-on- er, Full of peace and trust,   All his en - e-

sto- ry true, Hear him tell it all,   Heav - y chains are bind- ing him,
Mas-ter's name, To the Ro-man throne; Pomp and pow'r on ev - 'ry hand,
mies may scorn, Yet per-ish in the dust;   But His words of truth and pow'r,

In the court-room proud, But he does not fear the gaze Of the Grecian crowd.
But he does not quail, Speaking, for the cause of truth, Not a word shall fail.
Down the a- ges fall, " Dare to tell the sto- ry true, Dare to tell it all."

Chorus.

Dare   to be   a Paul, Dare to be   a Paul, Dare to tell the

sto - ry true and dare to tell it all;   dare to tell it all.

No. 99. SHALL I TURN BACK?

PSA. 23.

JAMES MONTGOMERY.   Arr. by H. H. HADLEY, 1895.

1. The Lord is my Shepherd, no want shall I know; I feed in green
2. Thro' the valley and shad-ow of death though I stray, Since Thou art my
3. In the midst of af - flic-tion, my ta - ble is spread With blessings un-
4. Let goodness and mer-cy, my boun-ti - ful God, Still fol - low my

pas - tures, safe fold - ed I rest: He lead - eth my soul where the
Guar-dian, no e - vil I fear, Thy rod shall de - fend me, Thy
num-bered, my cup run - neth o'er; With per-fume and oil Thou a-
steps till I meet Thee a - bove. I seek—by the path which my

still wa-ters flow, Re-stores me when wand'ring, re-deems when op-pressed.
staff be my stay: No harm can be - fall, with my Com - fort - er near.
noint-est my head: O what shall I ask of Thy prov - i - dence more?
fore - fa-thers trod Thro' the land of their so-journ, Thy Kingdom of love.

Chorus.

And shall I turn back in - to the world? Oh, no! not I! not I!

And shall I turn back in - to the world? No, no, not I!

From "Rescue Songs," used by permission of H. H. Hadley.

No. 100. O FOR A THOUSAND TONGUES.

AZMON. C. M.

CHARLES WESLEY.   LOWELL MASON.

1. O for a thou-sand tongues, to sing My great Re-deem-er's praise;

The glo-ries of my God and King, The triumphs of His grace!

2 My gracious Master and my God,
    Assist me to proclaim,
To spread thro' all the earth abroad,
    The honors of Thy name.

3 Jesus! the name that charms our
    That bids our sorrows cease; [fears,
'Tis music in the sinner's ears,
    'Tis life, and health, and peace.

4 He breaks the power of canceled sin,
    He sets the prisoner free;
His blood can make the foulest clean,
    His blood availed for me.

No. 101. *See music above.*

1 Salvation! O the joyful sound
    What pleasure to our ears?
A sovereign balm for every wound,
    A cordial for our fears.

2 Salvation! let the echo fly
    The spacious earth around,
While all the armies of the sky
    Conspire to raise the sound.

3 Salvation! O thou bleeding Lamb!
    To Thee all praise belongs :
Salvation shall inspire our hearts,
    And dwell upon our tongues.
              John Newton.

No. 102. *See music above.*

1 O for a heart to praise my God,
    A heart from sin set free!
A heart that always feels Thy blood,
    So freely spilt for me!

2 A heart resigned, submissive, meek,
    My great Redeemer's throne;
Where only Christ is heard to speak,
    Where Jesus reigns alone.

3 O for a lowly, contrite heart.
    Believing, true, and clean,   [part
Which neither life nor death can
    From Him that dwells within!

4 A heart in every thought renewed,
    And full of love divine,   [good,
Perfect, and right, and pure, and
    A copy, Lord, of Thine.
              Charles Wesley.

No. 103. *See music above.*

1 Am I a soldier of the cross,
    A follower of the Lamb,
And shall I fear to own His cause,
    Or blush to speak His name?

2 Must I be carried to the skies
    On flowery beds of ease,
While others fought to win the prize,
    And sailed through bloody seas?

3 Are there no foes for me to face?
    Must I not stem the flood?
Is this vile world a friend to grace,
    To help me on to God?

4 Sure I must fight, if I would reign;
    Increase my courage, Lord;
I'll bear the toil, endure the pain;
    Supported by Thy word.
              Isaac Watts.

CHRIST IS ALL.

"Unto you therefore which believe he is precious."—1 PET. 2 : 7.

To the memory of the late S. T. Gordon.

W. A. WILLIAMS.

1. I entered once a home of care, For age and pen-u-ry were there,
2. I stood be-side a dy-ing bed, Where lay a child with aching head.
3. I saw the mar-tyr at the stake, The flames could not his courage shake,
4. I saw the gos-pel her-ald go,—To Af-ric's sand and Greenland's snow,
5. I dream'd that hoary time had fled, And earth and sea gave up their dead,
6. Then come to Christ, oh! come to-day, The Fa-ther, Son, and Spir-it say,

Yet peace and joy withal; I asked the lone-ly mother whence Her helpless
Wait-ing for Je-sus' call; I mark'd His smile 'twas sweet as May, And as His
Nor death his soul appall, I ask'd Him whence his strength was giv'n, He look'd tri-
To save from Satan's thrall, Nor home nor life he counted dear 'Midst wants and
A fire dis-solved this ball, I saw the churche's ransom'd throng, I heard the
The Bride repeats the call, For He will cleanse your guilty stains His love will

Chorus.

wid-ow hood's defense, She told me "Christ was all,"
spir-it passed away, He whispered, "Christ is all."
umphantly to heav'n, And answered, "Christ is all."
perils owned no fear, He felt that "Christ is all."
burden of their song, 'Twas "Christ is all in all."
soothe your weary pains, For "Christ is all in all."

Christ is all, all in
Christ is all, all in

all, yes, Christ is all in all,
all. (Omit.) . . . . Yes, Christ is all in all.

No. 105. STAND UP, STAND UP FOR JESUS.

WEBB. 7s. 6s.

GEO. DUFFIELD.   GEO. WEBB.

1. { Stand up, stand up for Je-sus. Ye soldiers of the cross; }
   { Lift high your roy-al ban-ner, It must not (*Omit.*) . . } suf-fer loss:
D.C.—Till ev-'ry foe is vanquish'd, And Christ is (*Omit.*) . . Lord in-deed.

From vic - t'ry un - to vic - t'ry, His ar - my He shall lead,

2 Stand up, stand up for Jesus,
   The trumpet call obey;
Forth to the mighty conflict,
   In this His glorious day :
"Ye that are men, now serve Him,"
   Against unnumbered foes;
Your courage rise with danger
   And strength to strength oppose.

3 Stand up, stand up for Jesus,
   Stand in His strength alone;
The arm of flesh will fail you,
   Ye dare not trust your own;
Put on the gospel armor,
   Each piece put on with prayer,
Where duty calls, or danger,
   Be never wanting there.

No. 106. (*See music above.*)

1 The morning light is breaking;
   The darkness disappears;
The sons of earth are waking,
   To penitential tears :
Each breeze that sweeps the ocean,
   Brings tidings from afar;
Of nations in commotion,
   Prepared for Zion's war.

2 See heathen nations bending,
   Before the God of love,
And thousand hearts ascending,
   In gratitude above;
While sinners, now confessing,
   The gospel's call obey,
And seek a Saviour's blessing,
   A nation in a day.
9

3 Blest river of salvation,
   Pursue thy onward way;
Flow thou to every nation
   Nor in thy richness stay :
Stay not till all the lowly,
   Triumphant reach their home;
Stay not till all the holy
   Proclaim "The Lord is come!"

No. 107. (*See music above.*)

1 Unfurl the Temp'rance Banner,
   And fling it to the breeze,
And let the glad hosanna
   Sweep over land and seas ;
To God be all the glory
   For what we now behold—
Oh, let the cheering story
   In every ear be told.

2 The drunkard shall not perish
   In Alcohol's dire chain,
But wife and children cherish
   Within his home again;
And sobered men, repenting,
   Will bow at Jesus' feet.
Their thankful hearts relenting
   Before the mercy-seat.

3 A new-waked zeal is burning
   In this and every land,
And thousands now are turning
   To join our temp'rance band;
The light of truth is shining
   In many a darkened soul;
Ere long its rays combining
   Will blaze from pole to pole.

No. 108. Will You Meet Me at the Fountain?

N. G.

Nelson Gilreath, by per.

1. Will you meet me at the fount-ain, Where the crystal wa-ters flow?
2. Will you meet me at the fount-ain? Christ our Saviour bids you come;
3. Will you meet me at the fount-ain, Join the heav'nly choir a-bove?

Will you meet me at the fount-ain? You can wash as white as snow.
Will you meet me at the fount-ain? He'll prepare for you a home.
Will you meet me at the fount-ain? There where all is peace and love.

There we'll meet our lov-ing Sav - iour, Hear His gentle words of love;
Oth-er friends will give you wel - come, Ma - ny lov-ing hearts you'll cheer;
There'll be mu- sic at the fount-ain, Not a sor-row, not a tear;

And we'll live in sweet commun-ion With the saints in heav'n a-bove.
Won't you meet me at the fount-ain, At the fountain bright and clear?
Christ is wait-ing there to greet you; Won't you, won't you meet me there?

Will You Meet Me at the Fountain?—Concluded.

Chorus.

Yes, I'll meet you at the fount-ain With its waters bright and clear;

Oh, yes, I'll meet you, meet you;

Yes, I'll meet you at the fount-ain, Yes, I'll meet you, meet you there.

No. 109. THE COMING DAY.

1. { And must I be to judgment brought, And an-swer in that day }
   { For ev 'ry vain and i - dle thought, And ev - 'ry word I say? }

Chorus.

O what will you do in the com-ing day, In the coming day, the coming day;

When the heav'ns and the earth shall pass a-way, What will you do in that day?

2 Yes, every secret of my heart
  Shall shortly be made known,
And I receive my just desert
For all that I have done.—Cho.

3 How careful then ought I to live,
  With that religious fear;
Who such a strict account must give
For my behaviour here.—Cho.

4 Thou awful Judge of quick and dead,
  The watchful power bestow;
So shall I to my ways take heed,—
To all I speak or do.—Cho.

5. If now Thou standest at the door,
  O let me feel Thee near;
And make my peace with God, before
I at Thy bar appper.—Cho.

No. 110. *Music No. 1..*

1 See Jesus Thy deciples see
  The promised blessing give,
Within Thy name we look to Thee,
Expecting to receive.

2 Thee we expect our faithful Lord
  Who in Thy name are joined;
We wait according to Thy Word,
Thee in the midst to find.

3 With us Thou art assembled here,
  But, O, Thyself reveal!
Son of the living God appear
Let us thy presence feel.

4 Breathe on us Lord, in this our day,
  And these dry bones shall live,
Speak peace into our hearts and say
The Holy Ghost receive.

WITNESS FOR CHRIST.

"Tell how great things the Lord hath done for thee."—MARK 5: 9.

TABOR.
G. TABOR THOMPSON.

1. Are you walk - ing with the Lord? Tell it out! Tell it out!
2. Does your heart beat hot with - in? Tell it out! Tell it out!
3. Do you love this sa - cred hour? Tell it out! Tell it out!
4. Is your hope of glo - ry bright? Tell it out! Tell it out!

Speak for Him a lov - ing word. Tell it out! Tell it out!
Are you saved from in - bred sin? Tell it out! Tell it out!
Have you sanc - ti - fy - ing power? Tell it out! Tell it out!
Are you liv - ing in the light? Tell it out! Tell it out!

He will all your be - ing fill, While you do His ho - ly will,
Does the bless - ing o - ver - flow? Then let all the peo - ple know;
Are you ev - 'ry whit made whole? Does He wit - ness with your soul?
Christ will then con - fess for you. In that land be - yond the blue!

Tho' you're tempted to keep still, Tell it out! Tell it out!
Wit - ness - es for Christ be - low, Tell it out! Tell it out!
Let the tes - ti - mo - ny roll, Tell it out! Tell it out!
'Tis your turn, what will you do. Tell it out! Tell it out!

Chorus.

Tell it out! Tell it out! Tell it
Tell it out! Tell it out!

WITNESS FOR CHRIST.—Concluded.

old, old sto - ry, Tell it out!   Tell it out! Tell it out! Tell it
                        Tell it out!

out!   Tell the old, old sto - ry, Tell it out!
    Tell · it out!   Tell it out!

No. 112.   CORONATION.

1. All hail the pow'r of Je - sus' name, Let an - gels prostrate fall;
2. Sin - ners whose love can ne'er for - get, The wormwood and the gall,
3. Let ev - 'ry kin-dred, ev - 'ry tribe, On this ter - res-trial ball.
4. Oh, that with yon - der sa - cred throng, We at His feet may fall,

Bring forth the roy - al di - a - dem, And crown Him Lord of all;
Go spread your trophies at His feet, And crown Him Lord of all;
To Him all ma - jes - ty as-cribe, And crown Him Lord of all;
We'll join the ev - er - last - ing song, And crown Him Lord of all;

Bring forth the roy - al di - a - dem, And crown Him Lord of all.
Go spread your trophies at His feet, And crown Him Lord of all.
To Him all ma - jes - ty as- cribe, And crown Him Lord of all.
We'll join the ev - er - last - ing song, And crown Him Lord of all.

No. 113. THE LOYAL ARMY.

"Out of weakness were made strong, waxed valiant in fight."—Heb. 11: 34.

W. C. Brown, Arr. by W. A. O.   A. B. Kaufman, Arr. by W. A. O.

1. We've en- list- ed in the ar - my, in the ar - my of the Lord,
2. In this grand and glorious ar - my there is room for ev - 'ry one,
3. Let us march a-long to-geth - er, com-rades, fear- less-ly and bold,

We will la - bor in His ser- vice and o - bey His ho - ly word;
Who will wear the gos - pel ar - mor and go march-ing bravely on;
Loy - al sol- diers of the le - gion like the pa - tri-archs of old;

We will gath - er up the fragment here that noth-ing may be lost,
If you can- not preach the gos- pel, you a word for Christ can say
Let us swell the joy - ful cho - rus in a song of loud acclaim,

For the pre-cious blood of Je - sus paid the fear - ful cost.
To en - cour- age lit - tle sol- diers now up - on the way.
Hal - le - lu - jah, hal - le - lu - jah to the Sav - iour's name.

Chorus.

March - ing on . . . . so glad and free, . . . March- ing
March-ing on so glad and free,

By permission.

THE LOYAL ARMY.—Concluded.

to . . . the heav-'nly Canaan we, There to rest . . . from toil and
To the heav'n-ly   There to rest   from

care,   In that bless- ed promised land so bright and fair.
toil and care,   so fair.

No. 114.   PLEYEL'S HYMN.   7s.

IGNACE PLEYEL.

FINE.   D.S.

No. 115. Gracious Spirit, Love Divine.
See music above.

1 Gracious Spirit, love divine,
   Let Thy light within me shine!
   All my guilty fears remove;
   Fill me with Thy heavenly love.

2 Speak Thy pardoning grace to me;
   Set the burdened sinner free;
   Lead me to the Lamb of God;
   Wash me in His precious blood.

3 Life and peace to me impart;
   Seal salvation on my heart;
   Breathe Thyself into my breast,
   Earnest of immortal rest.

4 Let me never from Thee stray;
   Keep me in the narrow way;
   Fill my soul with joy divine;
   Keep me, Lord, forever Thine.
                        J. STOCKER.

No. 116. Holy Ghost, with Light Divine.
See music above.

1 Holy Ghost, with light divine,
   Shine upon this heart of mine;
   Chase the shades of night away,
   Turn my darkness into day.

2 Holy Ghost, with power divine,
   Cleanse this guilty heart of mine;
   Long hath sin, without control,
   Held dominion o'er my soul.

3 Holy Ghost, with joy divine,
   Cheer this saddened heart of mine;
   Bid my many woes depart,
   Heal my wounded, bleeding heart.

4 Holy Spirit, all divine,
   Dwell within this heart of mine;
   Cast down every idol-throne,
   Reign supreme—and reign alone.

No. 117.   ANTIOCH.

No. 118.   LENOX.

No. 119.   ROCKINGHAM.

No. 120. *Music No. 117.*

1 Joy to the world! the Lord is come;
   Let earth receive her King;
   Let every heart prepare Him room,
   And heaven and nature sing.

2 Joy to the world! the Saviour reigns;
   Let men their songs employ;
   While fields and floods, rocks, hills and
   Repeat the sounding joy.   [plains,

3 No more let sin and sorrow grow,
   Nor thorns infest the ground;
   He comes to make His blessings flow
   Far as the curse is found.

4 He rules the world with truth and grace
   And makes the nations prove
   The glories of His righteousness,
   And wonders of His love.

No. 121. *Music No. 118.*

1 Arise, my soul, arise;
   Shake off thy guilty fears;
   The bleeding sacrifice
   In my behalf appears;
   Before the throne my surety stands,
   My name is written on His hands.

2 He ever lives above
   For me to intercede,
   His all-redeeming love,
   His precious blood to plead;
   His blood atoned for all our race,
   And sprinkles now the throne of
   grace.

3 The Father hears Him pray,
   His dear annointed one;
   He can not turn away
   The presence of His Son;
   His Spirit answers to the blood,
   And tells me I am born of God.

4 My God is reconciled;
   His pard'ning voice I hear;
   He owns me for his child;
   I can no longer fear;
   With confidence I now draw nigh,
   And Father, Abba, Father, cry.

No. 122. *Music No. 118.*

1 Blow ye the trumpet, blow,
   The gladly solemn sound;
   Let all the nations know,
   To earth's remotest bound.
   The year of jubilee is come;
   Return, ye ransomed sinners, home.

2 Jesus, our great High Priest,
   Hath full atonement made;
   Ye weary spirits, rest;
   Ye mournful souls, be glad;
   The year of jubilee is come;
   Return, ye ransomed sinners, home.

3 Extol the Lamb of God,—
   The all-atoning Lamb;
   Redemption in His blood
   Throughout the world proclaim;
   The year of jubilee is come;
   Return, ye ransomed sinners, home.

No. 123. *Music No. 119.*

1 While life prolongs its precious light,
   Mercy is found and peace is given;
   But soon, ah, soon, approaching night
   Shall blot out every hope of heaven.

2 While God invites, how blest the day!
   How sweet the Gospel's charming
   sound!
   Come, sinners, haste, O haste away,
   While yet a pardoning God is found.

3 Soon, borne on times' most rapid wing,
   Shall death demand you to the grave,
   Before His bar your spirit bring,
   And none be found to hear or save.

4 In that lone land of deep despair,
   No Sabbath's heavenly light shall
   rise,
   No God regard your bitter prayer,
   No Saviour call you to the skies.

No. 124. BEYOND THE GRAVE.
(Can be sung to tune. 'Flowers from Angel Mother's Grave.")

1 In the days long gone by when your
   childish play was done,
   And you knelt down beside mother's chair,
   Little did you think that in days that
   soon would come
   You would leave mother's God and
   mother's prayer.
   But you left your home, and mother's
   heart was broken when you fell,
   When she saw the demons chain
   you; as a slave
   And the lips that kissed her darling
   when the evening prayers were
   said;
   For long years have been mouldering
   in the grave.

CHORUS.
   Onward you are drifting, drifting day
   by day,
   Soon, you will sink beneath the wave,
   Will you meet those gone before,
   On that happy golden shore,
   Or be banished from their home, be-
   yond the grave?

2 As they knelt by her side there to hear
   the last good-bye
   From the lips that once kissed away
   your care,
   Came the last whispering words as she
   pointed toward the sky:
   "Tell my loved ones to meet me over
   there."
   Death's cold waters rose around her as
   the life stream ebbed away,
   Then the Boatman came and took
   her 'cross the wave;
   Though the mists now hide her from
   you, still she's waiting over there.
   Will you meet her again beyond the
   grave.

No. 126. ORTONVILLE.

No. 127. GUIDE.

D.C.

No. 128.   *Music No. 125.*

1 My faith looks up to Thee,
. Thou Lamb of Calvary,
    Saviour divine;
Now hear me while I pray,
Take all my guilt away,
O let me from this day
    Be wholly thine.

2 May thy rich grace impart
Strength to my fainting heart,
    My zeal inspire;
As Thou hast died for me,
O may my love to Thee
Pure, warm, and changeless be—
    A living fire.

3 While life's dark maze I tread,
And griefs around me spread.
    Be Thou my guide;
Bid darkness turn to day,
Wipe sorrow's tear away,
Nor let me ever stray
    From thee aside.

No. 129.   *Music No. 125.*

1 My country! 'tis of thee,
Sweet land of liberty,
    Of thee I sing;
Land where my fathers died!
Land of the pilgrim's pride!
From every mountain side
    Let freedom ring!

2 My native country thee,
Land of the noble, free,
    Thy name I love;
I love thy rocks and rills,
Thy woods and templed hills:
My heart with rapture thrills
    Like that above.

3 Our father's God! to Thee,
Author of liberty,
    To Thee we sing;
Long may our land be bright
With freedom's holy light;
Protect us by Thy might,
    Great God, our King!

No. 130.   *Music No. 127.*

1 Holy Spirit, faithful Guide,
Ever near the Christian's side,
Gently lead us by the hand,
Pilgrims in a desert land.
Weary souls fore'er rejoice,
While they hear that sweetest voice,
Whisp'ring softly, wanderer, come!
Follow me, I'll guide thee home.

2 Ever present, truest friend,
Ever near, thine aid to lend,
Leave us not to doubt and fear,
Groping on in darkness drear.
When the storms are raging sore,
Hearts grow faint and hopes give o'er
Whisper softly, wanderer, come!
Follow me, I'll guide thee home.

No. 131.   *Music No. 126.*

1 How sweet the name of Jesus sounds
In a believer's ear!
It soothes his sorrow, heals his wounds
And drives away his fear.

2 It makes the wounded spirit whole,
And calms the troubled breast;
' Tis manna to the hungry soul,
And to the weary rest.

3 Till then I would thy love proclaim
With every fleeting breath;
And may the music of Thy name
Refresh my soul in death.

No. 132.   *Music No. 126.*

1 Oh for a faith that will not shrink,
Though pressed by every foe,
That will not tremble on the brink
Of any earthly woe;—

2 A faith that shines more bright and
When tempests rage without;[clear
That when in danger knows no fear,
In darkness feels no doubt;—

3 A faith that keeps the narrow way
Till lifes last hour is fled,
And with a pure and heavenly ray
Illumes a dying bed.

No. 133.   *Music No. 126.*

1 O for a closer walk with God,
A calm and heavenly frame;
A light to shine upon the road
That leads me to the Lamb!

2 Where is the blessedness I knew,
When first I saw the Lord?
Where is the soul-refreshing view
Of Jesus and His word?

3 Return, O holy dove, return,
Sweet messenger of rest!
I hate the sins that made Thee mourn
And drove Thee from my breast.

4 The dearest idol I have known,
Whate'er that idol be.
Help me to tear it from my throne,
And worship only Thee.

No. 134.   AUTUMN.

No. 135.   TOPLADY.

No. 136.   WOODWORTH.

W. B. BRADBURY.

No. 137. *Music No. 134.*

1 Hark, the voice of Jesus crying,
"Who will go and work to-day?
Fields are white and harvest waiting,
Who will bear the sheaves away?"
Loud and strong the Master calleth;
Rich reward He offers thee;
Who will answer gladly saying,
"Here am I; send me, send me."

2 Let none hear you idly saying,
"There is nothing I can do,"
While the souls of men are dying,
And the Master calls for you.
Take the task He gives you gladly;
Let His work your pleasure be;
Answer quickly when He calleth,
"Here am I, send, me, send me!"

No. 138. *Music No. 135.*

1 Rock of Ages cleft for me,
Let me hide myself in Thee
Let the water and the blood,
From Thy wounded side which flow'd
Be of sin the double cure;
Save from wrath, and make me pure.

2 Could my tears forever flow—
Could my zeal no languor know—
These for sin could not atone;
Thou must save and Thou alone;
In my hand no price I bring;
Simply to Thy cross I cling.

3 While I draw this fleeting breath,
When my eyes shall close in death,
When I rise to worlds unknown,
And behold Thee on Thy throne—
Rock of Ages, cleft for me,
Let me hide myself in Thee.

No. 139. Down at the Saviour's Feet.
Tune—Down by the Old Mill Stream.

1 I'm glad I ever heard the blessed story
Of love so full and free,
That gave up all of Heaven and its
glory,
And bore all the sufferings for me;
I'm glad that ere with broken heart
I sought the mercy seat,
And found relief from my load of sin
and grief,
While kneeling at the Saviour's feet.
Praise the Lord,

CHORUS.
Down at the Saviour's feet,
Love finds its heaven all complete;
Burdens roll away—
Darkness turns to day,
While kneeling at the Saviour's feet.

2 The world with all its joys no longer
charms me,
For purer bliss is mine;
The tempter with his darts no longer
harms me,

While kept by the power that's
divine,
From inward strife and fear set free;
My victory is complete.
In joy or pain, in earthly loss or gain,
I have heaven at the Saviour's feet.
Praise the Lord, etc.

No. 140. *Music No. 136.*

1 Just as I am without one plea,
But that Thy blood was, shed for me.
And that Thou bidst me come to Thee
O, Lamb of God, I come, I come!

2 Just as I am, and waiting not
To rid my soul of one dark blot, [spot
To Thee whose blood can cleanse each
O, Lamb of God, I come, I come!

3 Just as I am, thou wilt receive,
Wilt welcome, pardon, cleanse, relieve,
Because Thy promise I believe,
O, Lamb of God, I come, I come!

4 Just as I am, Thy love unknown,
Has broken every barrier down;
Now to be Thine, yea, Thine alone,
O Lamb of God, I come, I come!

No. 141. *Music No. 136.*

1 Lord, I am Thine, entirely Thine,
Purchased and saved by blood divine
With full consent Thine I would be
And own Thy sovereign right in me.

2 Grant one poor sinner more a place
Among the children of Thy grace;
A wretched sinner, lost to God,
But ransomed by Immanuel's blood.

3 Thine would I live, Thine would I die
Be Thine through all eternity:
The vow is past beyond repeal,
And now I set the solemn seal.

4 Here, at the cross where flows the blood
That bought my guilty soul for God,
Thee, my new Master, now I call,
And consecrate to Thee my all,

No. 142. *Music No. 134.*

1 Love divine all love excelling,
Joy of heaven to earth come down;
Fix in us Thy humble dwelling;
All Thy faithful mercies crown;
Jesus Thou art all compassion,—
Pure, unbounded love Thou art;
Visit us with Thy salvation;
Enter every trembling heart.

2 Come, almighty to deliver,
Let us all Thy life receive;
Suddenly return, and never,
Never more Thy temples leave;
Thee we would be always blessing,
Serve Thee as Thy hosts above,
Pray and praise Thee without ceasing
Glory in Thy perfect love.

No. 143. Must Jesus Bear the Cross Alone?

MAITLAND. C. M.

THOS. SHEPHERD.   GEO. N. ALLEN.

1. Must Je - sus bear the cross a - lone, And all the world go free?—

No; there's a cross for ev - 'ry one, And there's a cross for me.

2 The consecrated cross I'll bear,
  Till death shall set me free,
And then go home my crown to wear,
  For there's a crown for me.

3 Upon the crystal pavement, down
  At Jesus' piercèd feet,
Joyful, I'll cast my golden crown,
  And His dear name repeat.

4 O precious cross! O glorious crown!
  O resurrection day!
Ye angels from the stars come down,
  And bear my soul away.

No. 144. *See music above.*

1 Come, Holy Spirit, Heavenly Dove,
With all Thy quickening powers;
Kindle a flame of sacred love
In these cold hearts of ours.

2 Look how we grovel here below,
Fond of these earthly toys;
Our souls how heavily they go,
To reach eternal joys.

3 In vain we tune our formal songs
In vain we strive to rise;
Hosannas languish on our tongues,
And our devotion dies.

No. 145. *See music above,*

1 Jesus commands us to forgive
If we would be forgiven;
And Christians be while here on earth
Or reign with Him in heaven.

Cho.—I must forgive, I do forgive
  My every enemy;

For Jesus shed His precious blood
  That He might pardon me.

2 Tho' deeply wronged we may have been
  Our wrongs do not exceed
The insults we have heaped on Him
  Who for our sins did bleed.

3 He for His foes did suffer death,
  And freely all forgave;
And perished on the cruel cross
  That He their souls might save.

4 For those who pierced His hands and feet,
  Our Saviour prayed " Forgive ; "
His spirit we must all possess
  If we with Him would live.

5 O God, Thy Spirit now impart,
  That I Thine own may be;
That all my foes I may forgive
  As Thou forgivest me.

No. 146. *See music above.*

1 Amazing grace, how sweet the sound,
  That saved a wretch like me;
I once was lost, but now am found
  Was blind but now I see.

2 Thro' many dangers, toils and snares,
  I have already come;
'Tis grace has bro't me safe thus far,
  And grace will lead me home.

3 The Lord hath promised good to me,
  His word my hope secures;
He will my shield and portion be
  As long as life endures.

No. 147. I'M BELIEVING AND RECEIVING.

"Believing, ye rejoice with joy unspeakable."—1 PET. 1: 8.

H. H. R.   Commandant HERBERT BOOTH, by per.

mf Allegretto.

1. Sins of years are washed a-way, Blackest stains become as snow,
2. Doubts and fears are borne a-long On the cur-rent's ceaseless flow,
3. Ease and wealth become as dross, Worthless, earth's delight and show,
4. Self-ish - ness is lost   in love, Love for Him whose love you know,
5. Fighting is   a great de-light, Nev-er will you fear the foe,

Dark-est night   is changed to-day, When you to   the riv - er go.
Sor-row chang - es   in - to song, When you to   the riv - er go.
All your boast   is   in the cross, When you to   the riv - er go.
All your treas- ure is   a - bove, When you to   the riv - er go.
Armed by King Je- hovah's might, When you to   the riv - er go.

mf Chorus.

I'm be-lieving and receiving, While I to the riv-er go,   (Omit. . . .)
And my heart its waves are cleansing Whiter than (Omit. . .)   the driven snow.

No. 148.   HOW I LOVE THEE.

TUNE.—"*What a Friend we have in Jesus.*"

1 Precious Jesus, how I love Thee,
    Thou hast done so much for me,
  Thou hast pardoned my transgressions,
    Thou hast given liberty.
  Precious Jesus, I will trust Thee,
    When I'm tempted and oppressed,
  Thy great hand will keep me safely,
    Till the storm has o'er me passed.

2 Precious Jesus, Thou hast bought me—
    Bought me with Thy precious blood;
  I belong to Thee, dear Saviour,
    I belong to Thee, my God.

  I am Thine to do Thy bidding,
    Thine to go where Thou dost send,
  Thine to tell to those in darkness,
    Thou art every sinner's friend.

3 Light is found alone in Jesus;
    Christ, our Everlasting Light,
  Shine into these hearts, oh, Saviour,
    Turning darkness into light.
  Help us. Lord, to be more watchful
    O'er our thoughts and actions too.
  While we keep our eyes on Jesus
    He will keep us ever true.

By M. LOUISA MILLS, New York.

No. 149. GOING HOME.

No. 150. REVIVE US AGAIN.

CHORUS.

No. 151. DELIVERANCE WILL COME.

ENGLISH.

CHORUS.

No. 152. *Music No. 149.*

1 My heavenly home is bright and fair;
Nor pain nor death can enter there;
Its glittering towers the sun outshine
That heavenly mansion shall be mine.

CHORUS.

I'm going home, I'm going home,
I'm going home to die no more;
To die no more, to die no more,
I'm going home to die no more.

2 My Father's house is built on high,
Far, far above the starry sky.
When from this earthly prison free,
That heavenly mansion mine shall be.

3 While here a stranger far from home,
Afflictions waves may round me foam;
Although like Lazarus, sick and poor,
My heavenly mansion is secure.

No. 153. *Music No. 150.*

1 We praise Thee, O God!
For the Son of Thy love,
For Jesus who died,
And is now gone above.

CHORUS.

Hallelujah! Thine the glory,
Hallelujah! Amen.
Hallelujah! Thine the glory,
Revive us again.

2 We praise Thee, O God!
For Thy spirit of light,
Who has shown us our Saviour,
And scatter'd our night.

3 All glory and praise
To the Lamb that was slain,
Who has borne all our sins
And has cleans'd ev'ry stain.

4 Revive us again;
Fill each heart with Thy love,
May each soul be rekindled
With fire from above.

No. 154. *Music No. 151.*

1 I saw a happy pilgrim,
In shining garments clad,
While traveling up the mountain,
His countenance was glad;
He had no cares nor burdens,
He'd laid them at the cross,
The blood of Christ, his Saviour,
Had cleansed him from all dross.

CHORUS.

Then palms of victory,
Crowns of glory,
Palms of victory,
We shall wear.

2 The summer sun was shining,
The sweat was on his brow,
His garments worn and dusty,

His step seemed very slow,
But he kept pressing onward,
For he was wending home;
Still shouting as he journeyed,
Deliverance will come:

3 I saw him in the evening,
The sun was bending low,
Had overtopped the mountain;
And reached the vale below;
He saw the golden city,
His everlasting home,
And shouted loud, Hosannah!
Deliverance will come.

No. 155. LOST AFTER ALL.

(Can be sung to tune " After the Ball.")

1 A little child is kneeling by his moth-
er's chair,
Softly repeating sweet words of prayer
" Dear Loving Jesus, Gentle and Mild
Look down, and bless me, thy little
child."
Long kneels the Mother, praying that
night,
" God bless my treasure, guide him a-
right"
List to his story, weep o'er his fall,
Through his own madness, lost after
all.

REFRAIN.

After the days of childhood;
After a Mother's prayer,
After the years of manhood,
Freighted with joys and cares;
After a thousand chances,
After the final call,
Bitter the wail of a spirit;
Lost after all.

2 Changed is the picture, years have
swiftly flown,
Sadly the mother waits all alone.
Waits for her darling where does he
roam,
Has he forgotten mother and home?
Hark, there's a footstep, surely, 'tis he,
Oh Heaven help her what does she see?
Inside he staggers, one groan, a fall;
Wrecked by the wine cup, lost after all.

3 Farther and farther from his Mother's
God,
Wanders he on in sins road so broad,
Till by the window one stormy night,
He finds her waiting lifeless and white;
Vainly the spirit strives for his soul,
Spurning his God he turns to the bowl
Angels in Heaven, weep o'er his fall,
Still unrepentant, lost after all.

No. 156. THE PRINCE OF MY PEACE.

Words by Rev. W. F. Crafts. Music by W. G. Fischer. By per.

1. I stand all be-wilder'd with wonder, And gaze on the o-cean of love;
2. I struggled and wrestled to win it, The blessing that setteth me free;
3. He laid His hand on me and heal'd me, And bade me be ev-'ry whit whole;
4. The Prince of my peace is now passing, The light of His face is on me;

And o-ver its waves to my spir-it Comes peace, like a heaven-ly dove.
But when I had ceas'd from my strug-gles, His peace Je-sus gave un-to me.
I touch'd but the hem of His garment, And glory came thrilling my soul.
But lis-ten, be-lov-ed. He speaketh: "My peace I will give un-to thee."

REFRAIN.

Th' cross now cov-ers my sins; The past is un-der the blood;

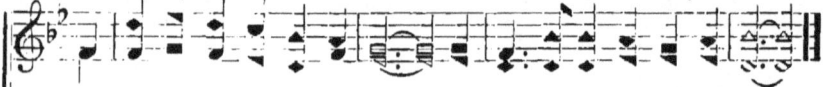

I'm trusting in Je-sus for all; My will is the will of my God.

No. 157. WE'LL WORK TILL JESUS COMES.

Mrs. Elizabeth Mills.

1 O land of rest, for thee I sigh,
When will the moment come,
When I shall lay my armor by
And dwell in peace at home?

Chorus.—
We'll work till Jesus comes,
We'll work till Jesus comes,
We'll work till Jesus comes,
And we'll be gather'd home.

2 No tranquil joys on earth I know,
No peaceful sheltering dome,

This world's a wilderness of woe,
This world is not my home.

3 To Jesus Christ I fled for rest;
He bade me cease to roam,
And lean for succor on his breast,
Till he conduct me home.

4 I sought at once my Saviour's side,
No more my steps shall roam;
With Him I'll brave death's chilling tide,
And reach my heavenly home.

No. 158.   I'LL BE THERE.   Old Melody.

1. { On   Jordan's stormy banks I stand, And cast a wish-ful eye
   { To   Canaan's fair and hap-py land, Where my po-ses-sions lie.

2. { O   the transport-ing, rapturous scene, That ris-es to my sight!
   { Sweet fields, arrayed in   liv-ing green, And riv-ers of de-light.

3. { There generous fruits that nev-er fail, On   trees im-mor-tal grow;
   { There rock, and hill, and brook, and vale, With milk and hon-ey flow.

3. { O'er   all those wide-ex-tend-ed plains, Shines one e-ter-nal day;
   { There God the Son for-ev-er reigns, And scat-ters night a-way.

Refrain.

I'll be there,   I'll be there, When the first trumpet sounds I'll be there.
I'll be there,   I'll be there,

I'll be there,   I'll be there, When the first trumpet sounds, I'll be there.
I'll be there,   I'll be there,

No. 159.   WE'LL WORK.

Chorus.

No. 160. THE GATES OF LIGHT SHALL OPEN.

IDA L. REED.   W. A. OGDEN.

1. Fear not thou care-worn one, Be pa - tient to the last,
2. Let this thy sad heart cheer, When by earth's cares op-pressed,
3. Tho' rough the way ap - pear, Be not dis-courag-ed, friend:
4. Let not thy cour-age fail, Though dark the path may be,

The tem - pest's heav - y frown Will van - ish —soon be past;
Thy feet are press-ing near The sweet e - ter - nal rest,
For God Him-self is near To suc - cor and de - fend,
Trust Him who said "my strength Suf - fi - cient is for thee."

Be - yond thy fee - ble sight, Where day reigns ev - er free,
Be - yond thy fee - ble sight, Where day reigns ev - er free,
Be - yond thy fee - ble sight, Where day reigns ev - er free,
Be - yond thy fee - ble sight, Where day reigns ev - er free,

Some day the gates of light, Will o - pen wide for thee.
Some day the gates of light, Will o - pen wide for thee.
Some day the gates of light, Will o - pen wide for thee.
Some day the gates of light, Will o - pen wide for thee.

The Gates of Light Shall Open. Concluded.

Refrain.

Some day, some day, some bright and glo-rious day
some day, some day,

The gates of light shall o - pen, Shall o - pen wide for thee.

No. 161. NEARER, MY GOD, TO THEE.

Mrs. SARAH F. ADAMS.

Scotch Air.

1. { Near-er, my God, to Thee! Nearer   to   Thee, } Still all my song shall be,
   { E'en tho' it be a cross That rais- eth   me ; }

2. { Tho' like a wan-der- er, The sun gone down, } Yet in my dreams I'll be
   { Darkness be o - ver me, My rest a stone, }

3. { There let the way appear, Steps un- to heaven. } An-gels to beck-on me
   { All that Thou sendest me, In mer-cy given; }

Near-er, my God, to Thee, Nearer, my God, to Thee, Nearer   to   Thee!

No. 162. Leaning on the Everlasting Arms.

Rev. E. A. Hoffman.

A. J. Showalter.

1. What a fel low-ship, what a joy divine, Lean-ing on the ev-er-
2. Oh, how sweet to walk in the pilgrim way, Lean-ing on the ev-er-
3. What have I to dread, what have I to fear, Lean-ing on the ev-er-

last - ing arms; What a bless - ed-ness, what a peace is mine,
last - ing arms; Oh, how bright the path grows from day to day,
last - ing arms? I have bless-ed peace with my Lord so near,

Refrain.

Lean - ing on the ev - er - last-ing arms.) Lean - ing
Lean - ing on the ev - er - last-ing arms. }
Lean - ing on the ev - er - last-ing arms.) Lean-ing on Je - sus,

lean - ing, Safe and se-cure from all a-larms;
lean - ing on Je - sus,

Lean - ing, lean - ing, Leaning on the ev-er-last-ing arms.
Leaning on Jesus, leaning on Jesus,

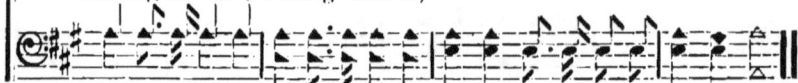

No. 163. REVIVE THY WORK, O LORD.

W. A. OGDEN.

1. Re - vive Thy work, O Lord, Thy might-y arm make bare,
2. Re - vive Thy work, O Lord, Cre - ate soul thirst for Thee,
3. Re - vive Thy work, O Lord, Ex - alt Thy pre-cious name,

Speak with the voice that wakes the dead, And make the peo- ple hear.
And hung'ring for the bread of life, O may our spir - its be.
And with the Ho - ly Ghost, our love For Thee, and Thine in - flame.

Refrain.

Re - vive Thy work, O Lord, And send re-fresh- ing showers,

The glo - ry shall be all Thine own, The blessing shall be ours.

No. 164   LOST ON THE MOUNTAINS.

JENNIE WILSON.   JAMES L. ORR.

1. O - ver sins mountains like sheep a-stray,   Pre-cious souls wan-der far,
2. "Lost on the mountains," oh hear the cry,   Quick to the res - cue, oh,
3. Climb the wild pathway so wild and steep,   Search thro' the val-ley so

far   a - way; Christ the Good Shepherd so patient and kind, Call-eth for
chris-tian fly! Help the Good Shepherd to gather the lost, Save them that
dark and deep, Seek for the straying ones thro' the dark night, Lov-ing-ly

Chorus.

help-ers the lost   to find.)
wan-der what-e'er the cost. } Ev - er in glo - ry the an-gel-songs roll,
lead them to Christ, the Light.)

When to the Sav - iour we bring a   lost soul, Sweeter and louder they

swell the glad sound, Tell-ing in glo - ry a   lost one is found.

No. 165. WITHOUT SPOT OR WRINKLE.

Eph. 5: 27.

CHARLIE D. TILLMAN.

1. Do you hear them com-ing, bro - ther, Thronging up the steeps of Light,
2. Do you hear the stir-ring An-thems, Fill - ing all the earth and sky?
3. Nev-er fear the clouds of sor - row, Nev - er fear the storms of sin,—
4. Wave the banner, shout His prais-es, For our vic - to - ry is nigh!

Clad in glo-rious shin-ing garments, Blood wash'd garments pure and white?
'Tis a grand vic - to - rious ar - my, Lift its ban - ner up on high.
We shall tri-umph on the mor-row, Ev - en now our joys be - gin.
We shall join our conquering Saviour, We shall reign with Him on high!

Chorus.

'Tis a glorious Church, without spot or wrin-kle, Wash'd in the blood of the Lamb,

'Tis a glorious Church, without spot or wrin-kle, Wash'd in the blood of the Lamb.

No. 166.   DON'T YOU WANT TO BE THERE?

E. R. LATTA.

JNO. R. BRYANT.

SEMI-CHORUS.

1. There's a land of wondrous beau - ty! Don't you want to be there?
2. There's a land of death-less pleas - ure, Don't you want to be there?
3. There's a land with cli - mate ver - nal! Don't you want to be there?
4. There's a land where saints are dwell - ing, Don't you want to be there?

SEMI-CHORUS.

'Tis the price of Christ-ian du - ty— Don't you want to be there?
And of ev - er - last-ing treas - ure—Don't you want to be there?
'Tis the realm of life e - ter - nal— Don't you want to be there?
They the love of Christ are tell - ing! Don't you want to be there?

Chorus.

How sweet 'twill be a - round His throne, To sing His praise with
loved ones gone For-ev - er to a- bide, In the heav - en - ly Je -
ru - sa-lem Where we shall know as we are known, Upon the other side.

No. 167. PRAISE HIM, HALLELUJAH!

Mrs. ADALINE H. BEERY.   Arr. by F. McD. H.

1. I learned a pre-cious se-cret, Low down at Je-sus' feet;
2. For once I was in dark-ness, And e-vil pressed me round;
3. No mat-ter how you've wronged Him, Tho' steeped in wick-ed-ness;

CHO.— O praise Him, hal-le-lu-jah! For love so full and free; O

Come to Him, dear troub-led soul, And hear the sto-ry sweet;
But when Je-sus called my soul, It was a wel-come sound;
Love and mer-cy beck-on still Your hum-ble soul to bless;

Lamb of God, who saves my soul, All praise I give to Thee;

If hap'-pi-ness you're seek-ing, He gives it full and free;
Now on the Rock of A-ges My feet se-cure-ly stand;
Come, kneel with all your bur-den Low down at Je-sus' feet;

Up-on the Rock of A-ges My feet se-cure-ly stand;

He'll take a-way your load of sin,—He's tak-en mine for me.
And day by day I sing my way Up t'ward the heav'nly land.
And when His par-don you re-ceive, The bless-ed news re-peat.

And day by day I sing my way Up t'ward the heav'nly land.

No. 168. ABIDING AND CONFIDING.

Rev. A. B. Simpson.   L. L. Pickett. By per.

1. I have learn'd the wondrous se-cret Of a-bid-ing in the Lord;
2. I am cru-ci-fied with Je-sus, And He lives and dwells in me,
3. All my cares I cast up-on Him, And He bears them all a-way;
4. For my words I take His wis-dom, For my works His Spir-it's power.

I have found the strength and sweetness Of con-fid-ing in His word;
I have ceas'd from all my struggling,'Tis no lon-ger I, but He;
All my fears and griefs I tell Him, All my needs from day to day,
For my ways His gra-cious Presence Guards and guides me ev-'ry hour,

I have tast-ed life's pure fountain, I am drink-ing of His blood,
All my will is yield-ed to Him, And His Spir-it reigns with-in,
All my strength I draw from Je-sus, By His breath I live and move,
Of my heart He is the Por-tion, Of my joy the cease-less Spring,

I have lost my-self in Je-sus, I am sink-ing in-to God.
And His pre-cious blood each moment Keeps me cleans'd and free from sin.
E'en His ver-y mind He gives me, And His faith, and life, and love.
Sav-iour, Sanc-ti-fi-er, Keep-er, Glo-rious Lord and com-ing King.

Chorus.

I'm a-bid - - - ing in the Lord, And con-
I'm a-bid-ing in the Lord, I'm a-bid-ing in the Lord, And con-

Copyright, 1891, by W. J. Kirkpatrick.

fid - - - ing in His word, And I'm hid - - -
fid - ing in His word, And con - fid - ing in His word, And I'm hid-ing, safe-ly

- - ing, safe-ly hid - - - ing, In the bos-om of His love.
hid-ing, I am hid-ing, safe-ly hid-ing,

No. 169. KNOWING.

Rev. M. W. KNAPP.   Rev. L. L. PICKETT.

1. Once I "wished" my sins were pardoned, And for - ev - er washed a -
2. Next, I "hoped" that all was set-tled, But my hopes were full of
3. Then I found that all be - liev - ers May sal - va - tion sure - ly
4. Now I "know" that Je - sus saves me, On His prom - is - es I

Cho. O this know so sal - va - tion, It is all the world to

Repeat for Chorus.

way, But the wish brought no as - sur-ance As I lingered day by day.
fear, Of- ten caus-ing sad de-pres-sion, And my way was nev -er clear.
* know, And re-joice in its pos-ses-sion, As they to the judgment go.
rest, And my soul is safe-ly an-chored In the ha - ven of His breast.

me, For it saves from con-dem-na-tion, And it makes me ful - ly free.

No. 170. LIFT ME HIGHER.

MAY CORNWELL.　　　　　　　　　　　　　　HAMP. H. SEWELL.

1. Lift me high-er, bless-ed Mas-ter, High-er still in - to the light,
2. Hold me clos- er, bless-ed Mas-ter, In　a firm and fond embrace,
3. Make me pur- er, bless-ed Mas-ter, Pure in pur-pose, deed and heart,

Up　a-bove the fear-ful shad- ows　Of earth's sin and gloom and night.
Let　no shadows pass between me　And the glo - ry　of　Thy face.
May the pur - i - ty　of　Je - sus　Of my own life form　a　part.

Chorus.

High - er,　Sav - iour,　Near - er　to　Thy pierc - ed side,
Lift me high- er, bless-ed Sav-iour,

With Thy lov-ing arms a - bout　me, Let me ev - er-more　a- bide.

No. 171. THE GOSPEL TRUMPET'S SOUNDING.

HAMP. H. SEWELL. by per.

1. The gos - pel trum-pet's sounding The year of ju - bi - lee;
2. For - sake your wretch-ed ser - vice, Your Mas-ter's claims are o'er;
3. A bet - ter Mas - ter's call.- ing, In ac- cents true and kind;
4. In liv - ing faith ac - cept him, Give up all else be - side.

And grace is all a - bond - ing, To set the bond-men free.
A - vail your selves of free - dom, Be Sa- tan's slaves no more.
He asks a lov - ing ser - vice, And claims a will - ing mind.
While grace is loud - ly call - ing, Look to the cru - ci - fied,

Chorus.

Re - turn, re- turn ye cap- tives, Re - turn un - to your home,

The gos - pel trum-pet's sound-ing, The ju - bi - lee is come.

Copyright, 1895, By Hamp. H. Sewell, Atlanta, Ga.

No. 172. JUST THE SAME TO-DAY.
See music 44, in The Revival.

1 Have you ever heard the story
   How our Lord before He died
Laid His blessed hands in healing
   Upon all who to Him cried,
How the sick and all oppressed ones
   He rejoicing sent away?
This He came to do, beloved,
   And He's just the same to-day.

2 Have you ever heard the story
   Of the Pentecostal day,
When the Holy Ghost descended,
   How He had the right of way?

And with cloven tongues of fire
   Inbred sin was swept away?
Oh, I'm glad, so glad to tell you
   He is just the same to-day.

3 Have you ever heard the promise
   That our risen Lord should come
Down to earth again and gather
   All His chosen people home?
Oh, He says He's surely coming,
   We must watch as well as pray;
God declares His word unchanging,
   He is just the same to-day.

No. 173. WAITING FOR HIS COMING.

Arranged.

HAMP. H. SEWELL, by per.

1. Oh so oft-en we are wea-ry 'Mid the hur-ry care and strife;
2. Like a bridegroom He is com-ing, Rescued souls will be His bride;
3. No more go-ing out for-ev-er, No more sor-row, no more tears,

And our souls are ev-er long-ing For the high-er bet-ter life;
Are our lamps all trimm'd and burning That we may with Him a-bide?
Death and pain can harm us nev-er, Thro' the glad e-ter-nal years.

When the tempest gath-ers 'round us, Oft, we lift our hearts and say:
In the ma-ny man-sions ho-ly Jeweled walls and streets of gold,
In the glo-ry of his pres-ence, Which now lights the Jasper sea;

I am wait-ing for Thy com-ing Bless-ed Je-sus night and day.
Gathered with the meek and low-ly, Safe for-ev-er in His fold.
We will meet the long-lost dear ones Waiting there for you and me.

Refrain.

We are wait - - - ing for His com - - - ing,
We are wait-ing, we are waiting for His com-ing, blessed com-ing.

And His prais-es we will sing,   We are   wait - - ing
hal-le-lulah! We are waiting, we are waiting

for the com - - ing   Of our Sav - iour, Lord and King.
for the com- ing, blessed com-ing

No. 174.   HE SAVES.

F. McD. H., arr.

1. Oh, Thou God of my sal - va- tion, My re-deem - er from all sin.
2. Tho' un-seen, I love my Sav-iour, He hath brought salvation near,
3. While the an - gel choirs are cry- ing, Glo - ry to the great I am,
4. An- gels now are hov'ring round us, Un- perceived a-mid the throng,

Cho.—Hal - le - lu - jah, hal - le - lu - jah, Hal - le - lu - jah, Je- sus saves,

Chorus D. C.

Moved by Thy di - vine compas - sion, Who hast died my heart to win.
Man - i- fests His pard'ning fav - or, And then Je - sus doth ap- pear.
I with them will still be vie - ing, Glo - ry, glo - ry to the Lamb.
Wond'ring at the love that crown'd us, Glad to join the love - ly song.

Yes, He saves me just at this mo- ment, Hal - le - lu - jah, Je - sus saves.

C. C. L.

C. C. LUTHER.

1. Beau - ti - ful hands at the gate-way to-night, Fa - ces all
2. Beck - on - ing hands of a moth- er whose love Sac - ri-ficed
3. Beau - ti - ful hands of a lit - tle one, see ! Ba - by voice
4. Beck - on- ing hands of a hus-band, a wife; Watch- ing and
5. Bright- est and best of that glo - ri - ous throng, Cen - ter of

shin - ing with ra - di - ant light; Eyes look-ing down from you
life her de - vo- tion to prove; Hands of a fa - ther to
call - ing oh, moth- er, for thee; Ro - sy-cheek'd darling, the
wait - ing the loved one of life ; Hands of a broth-er, a
all and the theme of their song. Je - sus, our Sav - iour, the

heav - en - ly home, Beau - ti - ful hands they are beck - on- ing "come."
mem - o - ry dear, Beck - on up high - er the wait- ing ones here.
light of the home, Tak - en so ear - ly, is beck - on-ing "come."
sis - ter, a friend, Out from the gateway to - night they ex - tend.
pierc - ed one stands, Lov - ing - ly call- ing with beck - on- ing hands.

Refrain.

Beau- ti-ful hands, beckoning hands, Calling the dear ones to heaven-ly lands:

Beau- ti-ful hands, beckoning hands, Beautiful, beauti-ful beckon-ing hands.

No. 176. THE RESURRECTION.

G. R. STREET. By per. of A. S. KIEFFER.

1. In the res-ur-rection morning We will see the Saviour coming, And the
2. We feel the ad-vent glory While the vision seems to tar-ry, We will
3. By faith we can dis-cov-er That our warfare'll soon be ov-er, And we'll
4. We will tell the pleasing story When we meet our friends in glo-ry, And we'll

CHORUS.

sons of God a-shouting in the kingdom of the Lord. We shall rise, we shall
comfort one anoth-er with the words of Ho-ly Writ.
shortly hail each other on fair heaven's hap-py shore.
keep ourselves already for to hail the heav'nly King. Hal-le-lu-jah!

When the trump of God shall sound, When the

rise! In the resurrection morning we shall rise!
Praise the Lord, Hal-le-lu-jah, Praise the Lord, we shall rise!

trump of God shall sound, It shall wake the sleeping nations, when the trump of God shall sound,

We shall rise, we shall rise! In the resurrection morning we shall rise!
Halle-lujah! Praise the Lord,

The dead in Christ shall rise, dead in Christ shall rise,

No. 177. OPENING SERVICE.

Sup't.—(*Rising.*) We praise Thee, O God, we acknowledge Thee to be the Lord.

School.—(*Rising.*) All the earth doth worship Thee, the Father everlasting.

Sup't.—To Thee all angels cry aloud; the heavens and all the powers therein.

Teachers.—To Thee Cherubim, and Seraphin continually do cry. (*Sing, Holy, Holy, etc.*)

HOLY, HOLY, LORD.

Response. *All sing.*   W. A. Ogden.

Ho - ly, Ho - ly, Lord, God Al - might - y ! All Thy

works shall praise Thee, in earth and sea and sky,

Ho - ly, Ho - ly, mer - ci - ful and might - y,

God in three per - sons, bless - ed Trin - i - ty.

Pastor.—The glorious company of the Apostles praise Thee.

Sup't.—The goodly fellowship of the Prophets praise Thee.

School.—The noble army of Martyrs praise Thee.

Pastor.—The holy church throughout the world doth acknowledge Thee; Thine adorable true and only Son; also the Holy Ghost, the Comforter.
(*Repeat "Holy, Holy, Lord, God Almighty," etc*)

No. 178. There's Nothing Between Me and Jesus.

L. E. J. L. E. JONES.

1. I've been to the fount-ain for cleansing from sin, There's noth-ing be-
2. My bur-den is gone since I came to His side, There's noth-ing be-
3. His shel-ter-ing hand o-ver-shad-ows my way, There's noth-ing be-
4. In mer-cy He sav'd me, and made me His own, There's noth-ing be-

tween me and Je-sus, His pres-ence is ev-er a-bid-ing with-in;
tween me and Je-sus, My soul is made free since His blood is ap-plied;
tween me and Je-sus, He leads me and keeps me by night and by day;
tween me and Je-sus, The King of my life He is reign-ing a-lone;

Chorus.

There's noth-ing between me and Je-sus.
There's noth-ing between me and Je-sus.
There's noth-ing between me and Je-sus.
There's noth-ing between me and Je-sus

There's nothing between, there's

nothing between, There's nothing between me and Je-sus; His word is a

light, making all my way bright, There's nothing between me and Je-sus.

No. 179. MAMMA KISSED ME IN A DREAM.

A thinly clad, ragged little girl boarded the cars alone. She was asked by the conductor where she was going. "Going to find mamma." "Where is your mamma?" "I don't know, they put her in a long, white box and carried her away on the cars, a long, long time ago. She kissed me last night in a dream and wanted me to come to where she was." The conductor, moved to tears, turned away as the little one lay down on the seat with her rag doll. She was soon asleep and slept only to wake up in heaven where she found her mamma.

J. R. B   JNO. R. BRYANT.

1. Mam - ma kissed me   in   a dream   last night, And she
2. In   a   long white   box they laid mam - ma, 'Twas a
3. 'Twas a   lit - tle   dream, im-pressed was she,   Its

bade me   come   a - way . . From the cares   of   life, From its
long, long time   a - go; . . From our home she's gone, Thro' those
bid - ding for   to   do; . . Just a   lit - tle while, The

toil and strife, To a brighter land than day;   With her snow-white arms a-
years slept on, And I don't know why 'tis so.   But they took her on the
tear, the smile, A - las! told it   was true.   For the sleep of death the

MAMMA KISSED ME, etc.—Concluded.

round my neck, As she used to long a - go, To her
ears a - way; Me and dol- lie must go on, Yet I
way re- vealed, Un - to her mam - ma's breast, There she

bo-som pressed, One that she loved best, 'Twas her "little pet," you know.
don't know where, But I know she's there, And awaiting us to come.
found that kiss, Perfect hap- pi-ness, With her mamma she was blest.

REFRAIN.

Mamma kissed me in a dream last night, As the an-gels hovered near,

In her sweet embrace, I could see her face, While her whisper I could hear.

No. 180.   I Am Satisfied with Jesus Here.

"They shall be abundantly satisfied with the fatness of thy house, and thou shalt make them drink of the river of thy pleasures." Ps. xxxvi: 8.
" He satisfieth the longing soul." Ps. cvii: 9.

M. W. KNAPP.   Arranged.

1. There's not a crav-ing of the mind   Which Je - sus can-not fill; . .
2. The joys which this vain world be-stows, Have lost their charms for me; . .
Cho. Yes, Je - sus sat - is - fies my soul,   He's more than all to me; . .

There's not   a pleasure I would seek   A - side from His dear will. . .
Once I   enjoyed its tri - fles too, . .   But Je - sus set me free. . .
For me   He shed His pre-cious blood,   And now I'm ful - ly free. . .

From hour to hour He fills my soul   With peace   and per-fect love;   While
His joys will perish in a   day.   Its pleas - ures quickly fly;   Its

Repeat for Chorus.

rich   sup-plies for ev - 'ry   need   He send - eth from a - bove. . . .
mirth like mist will pass a - way.   And all   its hon-ors die. . . .

3 But Jesus is my Saviour dear,
  My Rock, my Strength, my Song;
  My Wisdom and my Refuge Safe,
    To Jesus I belong.
  He is my Advocate with God,
    My Way, my Life, my Light,
  My Great Physician and my Friend,
    My Guide by day and night.

4 He stilled the angry tempests' power,
    Which raged within my heart;
  And bade each sinful passion there,
    To speedily depart.
  Yes, Jesus is my all in all,
    He satisfies my soul,
  For me He died on Calvary,
    And now He makes me whole.

No. 181. I'LL GO WITH HIM.

GEO. W. COLLINS. Arranged for This Work.

1. I have heard my Sav-iour calling, I have heard my Sav-iour call-ing,
2. Tho' He lead me thro' the val-ley, Tho' He lead me thro' the val-ley,
3. Tho' He lead me thro' the garden, Tho' He lead me thro' the garden,

CHO. *Where He leads me I will fol-low, Where He leads me I will fol-low,*

Repeat for Chorus.

I have heard my Sav-iour calling, "Take thy cross and follow, fol-low me."
Tho' He lead me thro' the val-ley, I'll go with Him, with Him all the way.
Tho' He lead me thro' the gar-den, I'll go with Him, with Him all the way.
Where He leads me I will fol-low, I'll go with Him, with Him all the way.

Arr. Copyrighted, 1894, by Jno. R. Bryant.

4 ‖: Tho' the path be dark and dreary, :‖
I'll go with Him, with Him all the way.

5 ‖: Tho' He lead me to the conflict, :‖
I'll go with Him, with Him all the way.

6 ‖: Tho' He lead thro' fiery trials, :‖
I'll go with Him, with Him all the way.

7 ‖: I will follow on to know Him, :‖
He's my Saviour, Saviour, Brother,
Friend.

8 ‖: He will give me grace and glory, :‖
He will keep me, keep me all the way.

9 ‖: Oh, 'tis sweet to follow Jesus, :‖
And be with Him, with Him all the way.

No. 182. "OLD TIME RELIGION."

Arr. CHARLIE TILLMAN.

CHO. 'T is the old time re-li-gion, 'T is the old time re-li-gion, 'T is the old time re-
1. It was good for our mothers, It was good for our mothers, It was good for our
2. Makes me love ev-'ry bod-y, Makes me love ev-'ry bod-y, Makes me love ev-'ry-
3. It has sav-ed our fa-thers, It has sav-ed our fa-thers, It has sav-ed our

li-gion, It's good enough for me.
mothers, It's good enough for me.
bod-y, It's good enough for me.
fathers, It's good enough for me.

4 :‖: It was good for the Prophet Daniel, :‖:
It's good enough for me.

5 :‖: It was good for the Hebrew Children, :‖:
It's good enough for me.

6 :‖: It was tried in the fiery furnace, :‖:
It's good enough for me.

7 :‖: It was good for Paul and Silas, :‖:
It's good enough for me.

8 :‖: It will do when I am dying, :‖:
It's good enough for me.

9 :‖: It will take us all to heaven, :‖:
It's good enough for me.

Copyright, 1891, by Charlie D. Tillman.

No. 183.   SALVATION IN THE HEART.

Arr. by E. L. K. and W. P.

1. I'm glad I have sal-va-tion In my heart, I'm
2. I want to be like Je-sus, In my heart, I
3. I will not be de-ceit-ful In my heart, I
4. I want to love my neighbor, In my heart, I
5. I want to love my ene-mies, In my heart, I
6. I feel the Spir-it burn-ing In my heart, I

In my heart,

glad I have sal-va-tion, In my heart, In my heart, In my
want to be like Je-sus, In my heart, In my heart, In my
will not be de-ceit-ful In my heart, In my heart, In my
want to love my neighbor, In my heart, In my heart, In my
want to love my ene-mies, In my heart, In my heart, In my
feel the Spir-it burn-ing In my heart, In my heart, In my

In my heart,

heart,   I'm glad I have sal-va-tion In my heart.
heart,   •   I want to be like Je-sus, In my heart.
heart,   I will not be de-ceit-ful In my heart.
heart,   I want to love my neigh-bor, In my heart.
heart,   I want to love my ene-mies, In my heart.
heart,   I feel the Spir-it burn-ing In my heart.

In my heart,

No. 184.   BRINGING IN THE SHEAVES.

1 Sowing in the morning, sowing seeds of kindness,
  Sowing in the noon-tide, and the dewy eves;
  Waiting for the harvest, and the time of reaping,
  We shall come rejoicing, bringing in the sheaves.

Cho.—Bringing in the sheaves, bringing in the sheaves,
      We shall come rejoicing, bringing in the sheaves.

2 Sowing in the sunshine, sowing in the shadows,
  Fearing neither clouds nor winter's chilling breeze,
  By and by the harvest, and the labor ended,
  We shall come rejoicing, bringing in the sheaves.

3 Go, then, even weeping, sowing for the Master,
  Though the loss sustained our spirit often grieves;
  When our weeping's over He will bid us welcome,
  We shall come rejoicing, bringing in the sheaves.

No. 185. JESUS LIVES!

(For Y. P. S. C. E. and Epworth Leagues.)

REV. JOHN R. COLGAN. A. F. MYERS.

1. Might-y ar- my of the young, Lift your voice in cheerful song, Send the wel-come
2. Tongues of children light and free, Tongues of youth and full of glee, Sing to all on
3. Je-sus lives, O blessed words! King of kings, and Lord of lords! Lift the cross and

word a - long, Je-sus lives! Once he died for you and me, Bore our sins upon the tree;
land and sea, Jesus lives! Light for you and all mankind, Sight for all by sin made blind;
sheathe the swords, Jesus lives! See, he breaks the prison wall, Throws aside the dreadful pall,

CHORUS.

Now he lives to make us free, Jesus lives! Wait not till the shadows lengthen, till you older grow,
Life in Je-sus all may find, Je-sus lives!
Conquers death at once for all, Jesus lives! Wait not,

Wait not, wait not,

Rally now and sing for Je - sus ev-'rywhere you go; Lift your joyful voices high,
Sing, sing,

Sing for Je - sus,

Repeat Chorus pp.

f rit.

Ring-ing clear thro' earth and sky, Let the bless -ed ti-dings fly, Je -sus lives!

Copyright, 1891, by A. F. Myers, Toledo, O.

No. 186. THE CRIMSON STREAM.

P. L. Harris.

Will M. Waller.
Har. by Charlie D. Tillman.

1. There is a crimson stream unseen, That flows from Cal-va-
2. Tho' full of en-vy, pride and lust, From these you may be

ry; There we thro' faith tho' all un-clean, May
poor; Come to this heal-ing stream in trust, The

D.S. A foun-tain of life for all man-kind, Go
FINE. CHORUS.

wash our sins a-way. Go wash in that beau-ti-ful
prom-is-es are sure.

wash in that beau-ti-ful stream.

D.S.

stream (beautiful stream), Go wash in that beau-ti-ful stream (beautiful stream);

3 There millions now in realms of light
Who once were vile as we;
Have washed their robes and made them white,
We too like them may be.

4 Come to this crimson stream to-day,
With all your guilt and sin;
O sinner, come, without delay,
And wash and be made clean.

No. 187. ALL THE WORLD FOR JESUS.

Dedicated to the Armstrong Co. C. E. Convention, Kittanning, Pa., 1895.

Mrs. FRANK A. BRECK.   GRANT C. TULLAR.

With vigor.

1. Take up the bat-tle-cry all a-long the line; Vic-to-ry
2. Truth's ar-mor you may claim, faith will be your shield; Fighting on in
3. Sol-diers, with courage go, go for-sak-ing all; Onward, then, to

by and by, vic-to-ry di-vine, With your commander nigh,
Je-sus' name mighty pow'r you wield; Glo-ry for God your aim,
meet the foe, soon the foe shall fall; Send might-y blow on blow,

foes in vain combine; Raise a-loft the ban-ner let it bear the sign.
naught can make you yield; Shout aloud the triumph sure to be revealed.
let no fear ap-pall; In the name of Je-sus sound a-far the call.

CHORUS.

"All the world for Je-sus," let the cho-rus ring; "All the world for

Je-sus," crown Him King: "All the world for Je-sus,"

let the watchword be "Forward go in Jesus' name to victory."

No. 188. PRECIOUS IS THE BLOOD.

G. C. T. 1 Peter 1: 18, 19. GRANT C. TULLAR.

1. Naught have I to make my plea, Precious is the cleansing blood;
2. While I wandered far in sin, Precious is the cleansing blood;
3. Once in sor-row sin and woe, Precious is the cleansing blood;
4. Till I see my Saviour King, Precious is the cleansing blood;

But that Je-sus died for me, Oh, precious is the cleansing blood.
Je-sus found and took me in, Oh, precious is the cleansing blood.
Now in paths of peace I go, Oh, precious is the cleansing blood.
Still my soul in joy shall sing, Oh, precious is the cleansing blood.

CHORUS.

Oh, the cleansing now I see, Je-sus shed His blood for me;

That applied now sets me free, Oh, precious is the cleansing blood.

INDEX.

INDEX.